VERBAL
REASONING
TESTS

how2become

Wolverhampton City Council	
X400 000000 3501 C3	
Askews & Holts	
153.94 53 mcm	£13.00
12.12.13	ALL

Orders: Please contact How2become Ltd,
Suite 2, 50 Churchill Square Business Centre, Kings Hill, Kent ME19 4YU. You can also order via the email address info@how2become.co.uk and at Gardners.com.

ISBN: 9781907558726

First published 2012

Typeset for How2become Ltd by Molly Hill, Canada.

Proofread for How2become Ltd by SmartThinker Solutions.

Printed in Great Britain for How2become Ltd by Bell & Bain Ltd, 303 Burnfield Road, Thornliebank, Glasgow G46 7UQ.

CONTENTS

INTRODUCTION

Before I started creating this workbook I sat down and thought about the type of information a reader would expect from such a book. After some careful deliberation I decided that the book would need to include tips and advice on how to improve performance when carrying out verbal reasoning tests, lots of sample test questions and also explanations as to how the answers are reached. I also felt that the workbook should consist of the type of questions a candidate is more than likely to come across during a job selection process in today's environment.

Verbal reasoning tests have been in use for many years as a tool by employers whilst assessing potential employees for specific careers. During my research, and whilst discussing this type of test with test administrators, I established that the most common type of verbal reasoning test in use today is the one that involves a passage of text and a requirement for the candidate to state whether certain statements relating to the passage are; true, false or cannot say from the information provided.

During my research I also encountered a small number of employers using tests which involved a requirement for the candidate to select the odd one out from a list of items, such as:

Select the odd one out from the following list

    Baby | Daylight | Cot

ANSWER: Daylight

I also encountered that some employers used the 'insert the missing word' form of verbal reasoning test as per the example below:

The following sentence has 2 words missing. Which two words make best sense of the sentence?

The man _____to walk along the beach with his dog. He threw the stick and the dog _____ it.

ANSWER:

A. hated/chose

B. decided/wanted

C. liked/chased

D. hurried/chased

E. hated/loved

ANSWER: C

I figured that, if I was to include questions of this nature within the work-book, many of you would give me a severe grilling in the reviews section on Amazon, simply because these questions are far too easy to answer for the majority of people. Having said that, I do believe these types of questions should be practised, if your assessment contains them. The reason why many of these 'simple' verbal reasoning tests are not being used anymore is because there is a requirement under employment law for the employer to use tests that are reflective of the work the successful candidate will be required to undertake in the role.

Some organisations such as the Armed Forces do still use select the odd one out tests. So, in order to meet the requirements of everyone, I have created an online testing suite which contains questions of the above nature. You are welcome to use the testing suite free of charge – simply go the following website to gain immediate free access to the questions:

www.verbalreasoningtestsonline.co.uk

This workbook will concentrate on the type and format more commonly found in the majority of career selection processes found today.

Verbal reasoning tests are usually timed and as such I recommend you carry out lots of practice under strict timed conditions. It is extremely difficult to replicate exact testing conditions during preparation; however, by preparing yourself in this manner you will be giving yourself the best chance of success. The time limit supplied in the majority of verbal reasoning tests is designed so that you find it impossible to complete the test. Those candidates who are unaware of this fact will often panic as they see the clock ticking away, yet their progress through the test does not match the quantity of time remaining. Yes it is important to work as fast as you can, but accuracy is also an essential element of your overall score. Tests are now far more advanced and sophisticated than they used to be. They give an accurate assessment of how a potential employee is likely to perform in a certain role.

The assessor/employer will get to see exactly how many questions you attempted, how many you got right and also how many you scored incorrectly. Within this workbook I will avoid advising you to 'guess' the final few questions if you notice that you only have a few seconds left at the end. Whilst talking to a number of assessors during my research it soon became apparent that some assessors will deduct marks for guessing or incorrect answers. Therefore, it is important that we concentrate on both speed and accuracy during this workbook.

ADVICE FOR IMPROVING YOUR SCORES

Develop an action plan
When preparing for your verbal reasoning tests implement an action plan of preparation. I recommend carrying out at least 30 minutes practice per day/evening in the fortnight before the test. The reason why I state a fortnight is simply because this is an approximate amount of time that the employer will give you to prepare before your test date. If you get longer to prepare, use the time wisely.

Time yourself from the outset
Prepare for the tests by using 'time' from the outset. This means timing yourself even when carrying out practice tests. Get used to the feeling of the clock ticking down and the pressure you will be under. Many people do not carry out practice tests under timed conditions. When it comes to real test day they suffer as a result. It is also important to be aware that you should

time yourself from the point that you start reading the verbal comprehension passage. Some people believe that the test only starts when you study the answer options; this is incorrect.

Have an organised mind-set

Develop an organised mind-set. There is a difference between a 'seasoned' test taker and a novice test taker. A seasoned test taker will approach the test in a formalised manner, whereas the novice will bluff his or her way through the test. Your approach to verbal reasoning tests should include the following:

1. The only way to gain high scores is to ensure that your mind and body are at their best. In the fortnight before the test avoid alcohol, cigarettes, coffee and junk food. Make a conscious effort to eat healthily, drink plenty of water and get plenty of sleep/rest.

2. A large percentage of test takers fail to follow the instructions provided at the commencement of the test. Listen to what the test administrator tells you. Most candidates are more concerned about the other test takers in the room rather than being concerned about the rules of the test. Focus on your own performance only and do not worry about anyone else in the room. Listen to what is being said and follow all instructions carefully. If you are unsure, ask.

Accurate marking is crucial

The vast majority of verbal reasoning tests are multiple-choice in nature. The main reason for this type of test is because it allows the employer/ assessor to score a large number of tests quickly. Because if this fact it is essential that you complete the marking sheet accurately. If you miss a question be sure to leave a space on the marking sheet. I have known of people to fail an entire test because they failed to leave a space on the marking sheet after missing out a question.

Pace yourself according to the allocated time

Just before the test commences the test administrator will inform you of how many questions there are within the test and also the time limit you have to complete it. This is your opportunity to provide yourself with an 'approximate' time to answer each question. For example, if you are informed that there are thirty questions in the test and you have 20 minutes to complete them, this gives you an average of forty seconds per question. If you find yourself spending up to two minutes on a question then you are probably spending far too much time trying to answer it.

Concentrate fully

During the test concentrate fully on the passage of text you are reading. It is pointless reading the passage unless you are concentrating fully on the content. It is very easy to get distracted, either by other test takers or by the time remaining.

Use an approach that suits you

I have found that the vast majority of people who take verbal reasoning tests approach them by reading the entire passage through once before turning to the questions. Personally, I prefer to read the question first and then scan the passage for 'keywords' and 'phrases' which match the question. The bottom line is this: there are no hard and fast rules for approaching the questions. Choose a method that works for you. I can guarantee you that you will have developed your own method for answering the questions by the time you have completed this workbook.

Answer the questions based solely on the information provided

Candidates who sit verbal reasoning tests often fall into the trap of answering the question based on fact, rather than answering the question based solely on the information provided in the text. I have already stated that the type of question you are likely to encounter will involve a passage of text followed by a series of questions which must be answered either TRUE, FALSE or CANNOT SAY based on the information given. Let me give you an example of how people fall foul of the CANNOT SAY option.

Read the following text before answering the question as either TRUE, FALSE or CANNOT SAY based on the information provided.

A uniform is a set of standard clothing worn by members of an organisation whilst participating in that organisation's activity. Modern uniforms are worn by armed forces and paramilitary organisations such as; police, emergency services and security guards, in some workplaces and schools and by inmates in prisons. In some countries, officials also wear uniforms in some of their duties; such is the case of the Commissioned Corps of the United States Public Health Service or the French Prefects.

Q. Police officers are required to wear a uniform.

The answer to the question is **CANNOT SAY** based on the information provided. Many candidates will answer this question as TRUE; simply because we all know that police officers do in fact wear a uniform. The important lesson here is to only answer the question based solely on the information provided, regardless of what you know to be fact.

A SAMPLE VERBAL REASONING TEST QUESTION AND HOW TO APPROACH IT

Let's now take a look at a sample verbal reasoning test question in a format which is common amongst employers nowadays.

You will normally find a passage of text which is followed by a number of questions. Following the questions you are required to state whether the questions are **TRUE, FALSE,** or **CANNOT SAY** without further information.

Read the following text before answering the questions as either TRUE, FALSE or CANNOT SAY from the information given.

BASIC HOLIDAY RIGHTS FOR EMPLOYEES

There is a minimum right to paid holiday, but your employer may offer more than this. All employees are entitled to a minimum of 5.6 weeks paid leave per year. Those employees who work for five days a week are entitled to 28 days per year annual leave (capped at a statutory maximum of 28 days for all working patterns). Employees who work part-time are entitled to the same level of holiday pro rata (5.6 times your normal working week) e.g. 16.8 days for someone working three days a week. All employees will start building up holiday entitlement as soon as they start work with the employer.

The employer has the right to control when you take your holiday but you must get paid the same level of pay whilst on holiday. When you finish working for an employer you get paid for any holiday you have not taken. The employer may include bank and public holidays in your minimum entitlement.

You continue to be entitled to your holiday leave throughout any additional maternity/paternity leave and adoption leave.

---

1. An employer may not offer you more than the minimum paid holiday.

2. In addition to paternity leave you are entitled to your normal holiday.

3. All employees only start building up holiday leave 5.6 weeks after commencement of employment.

4. Employees who receive more than the minimum holiday entitlement are often grateful to their employer.

The above sample question consists of a passage of text which relates to basic holiday rights for employees followed by four questions. You have to state whether the questions are either TRUE, FALSE or CANNOT SAY from the information given. The important thing to remember is that you should solely base your answers on the passage of text provided. Let's break each question down individually:

1. An employer may not offer you more than the minimum paid holiday.

By reading the passage carefully you will note that the following sentence relates to Question 1:

"There is a minimum right to paid holiday, but your employer may offer more than this."

We can deduce from the passage that Question 1 is in fact **FALSE**, simply because an employer may offer more than the minimum paid holiday.

Fortunately for us the first question related to the very first sentence in the passage. However, in the majority of cases this will not be the norm.

2. In addition to paternity leave you are entitled to your normal holiday.

By reading the passage carefully you will note that the following sentence relates to Question 2:

"You continue to be entitled to your holiday leave throughout any additional maternity/paternity leave and adoption leave."

We can deduce from the passage that Question 2 is in fact **TRUE**. An employee is entitled to their holiday leave throughout paternity leave.

I previously stated that my preferred method for answering verbal reasoning questions was to scan the passage searching for keywords or phrases which matched the question. Question 2 is a very good example of how 'scanning' the passage can save you time. You will note that the word 'paternity' is only used once throughout the entire passage. By scanning the passage quickly in search of specific keywords or phrases you will be able to reach the section of the passage that relates to the question and thus answer the question far quicker than reading the entire passage.

Once again, there is no right or wrong way for answering the questions; choose a method which works for you.

3. All employees only start building up holiday leave 5.6 weeks after commencement of employment.

By reading the passage carefully you will note that the following sentence relates to Question 3:

"All employees will start building up holiday as soon as they start work with the employer."

We can deduce from the passage that Question 3 is in fact **FALSE** based on the information provided. An employee starts building up holiday as soon as they start work with the employer, not 5.6 weeks after commencement of employment.

4. Employees who receive more than the minimum holiday entitlement are often grateful to their employer.

By reading the passage carefully you will note that none of the content relates to the question. At no point does it state that employees who receive more than the minimum holiday entitlement are often grateful to their employer, or otherwise. Therefore, the answer is **CANNOT SAY** based on the information provided. Although it is probably true in real life that most employees would be grateful for receiving more than the minimum holiday requirement, we can only answer the question based solely on the information provided in the passage.

I now want you to try the five sample questions that follow. Take your time when answering the question as there is no time limit for these specific questions. The answers/explanations are provided following each question.

1. Read the following text before answering the questions as either TRUE, FALSE or CANNOT SAY from the information given.

WINTER FUEL PAYMENTS

Members of the public may get a Winter Fuel Payment for winter if they have reached the qualifying age (born on or before 5 January 1951) and you also normally live in Great Britain or Northern Ireland on any day in the week of 19–25 September 2011. They won't qualify for a Winter Fuel Payment if, throughout the week of 19–25 September 2011, they were in hospital for more than 52 weeks previously, getting free treatment as an in-patient.

They will also not qualify if they were in custody serving a court sentence, were subject to immigration control and did not qualify for help from the Department for Work and Pensions, lived in a care home, an independent hospital, income-based Jobseeker's Allowance or income-related Employment and Support Allowance.

In addition to these restrictions you cannot qualify for a Winter Fuel Payment if you move to another European Economic Area country or Switzerland and did not qualify before you moved.

Winter Fuel Payment is paid for the household and you will be paid directly into your bank account or by cheque depending on which format you requested.

A – TRUE	B – FALSE	C – CANNOT SAY
Circle A if the question is TRUE from the information provided.	Circle B if the question is FALSE from the information provided.	Circle C if CANNOT SAY from the information provided.

1. You can qualify for a Winter Fuel Payment if you move to France.

A   B   C

2. Winter Fuel Payment can <u>only</u> be paid directly in your bank account.

A   B   C

3. Members of the public will not qualify for a Winter Fuel Payment if, throughout the week of 19–25 September 2011, they were in a care home.

A   B   C

REVIEW YOUR ANSWERS

1. Read the following text before answering the questions as either TRUE, FALSE or CANNOT SAY from the information given.

WINTER FUEL PAYMENTS

Members of the public may get a Winter Fuel Payment for winter if they have reached the qualifying age (born on or before 5 January 1951) and you also normally live in Great Britain or Northern Ireland on any day in the week of 19–25 September 2011. They won't qualify for a Winter Fuel Payment if, throughout the week of 19–25 September 2011, they were in hospital for more than 52 weeks previously, getting free treatment as an in-patient.

3: They will also not qualify if they were in custody serving a court sentence, were subject to immigration control and did not qualify for help from the Department for Work and Pensions, lived in a care home, an independent hospital, income-based Jobseeker's Allowance or income-related Employment and Support Allowance.

In addition to these restrictions 1: you cannot qualify for a Winter Fuel Payment if you move to another European Economic Area country or Switzerland and did not qualify before you moved.

2: Winter Fuel Payment is paid for the household and you will be paid directly into your bank account or by cheque depending on which format you requested.

REVIEW YOUR ANSWERS

A – TRUE	**B – FALSE**	**C – CANNOT SAY**
Circle A if the question is TRUE from the information provided.	Circle B if the question is FALSE from the information provided.	Circle C if CANNOT SAY from the information provided.

1. You can qualify for a Winter Fuel Payment if you move to France.

A   B   C

The passage states *"you cannot qualify for a Winter Fuel Payment if you move to another European Economic Area country"*. The statement is, therefore, **false**.

2. Winter Fuel Payment can only be paid directly in your bank account.

A   B   C

The statement is **false** because the passage states *"Winter Fuel Payment is paid for the household and you will be paid directly into your bank account or by cheque depending on which format you requested"*.

3. Members of the public will not qualify for a Winter Fuel Payment if, throughout the week of 19–25 September 2011, they were in a care home.

A   B   C

The passage confirms the statement to be **true**.

2. Read the following text before answering the questions as either TRUE, FALSE or CANNOT SAY from the information given.

ANIMAL EUTHANASIA

Animal euthanasia is the practice of terminating the life of an animal in a painless or minimally painful way in order to stop suffering or other unde-sired conditions in life.

This may be voluntary or involuntary, and carried out with or without a physician. In a medical environment, this can be carried out by oral, intra-venous or intramuscular drug administration. Laws around the world vary greatly with regard to animal euthanasia and are constantly subject to change as cultural values shift and better palliative care or treatments become available. Reasons for animal euthanasia include:

- Terminal illness – eg cancer.

- Rabies.

- Behavioural problems (that usually cannot be corrected) – e.g. aggression.

- Illness or broken limbs that would cause suffering for the animal to live with, or when the owner cannot afford (or has a moral objection to) treatment.

- Old age – Deterioration to loss of major bodily functions. Severe impairment of the quality of life.

- Lack of homes – Some shelters receive considerably more sur-rendered animals than they are capable of re-housing. This may be attributed to irresponsible owners who do not spay or neuter pets, causing unwanted litters. Some pets turned in to animal shelters are not adopted out.

A – TRUE	B – FALSE	C – CANNOT SAY
Circle A if the question is TRUE from the information provided.	Circle B if the question is FALSE from the information provided.	Circle C if CANNOT SAY from the information provided.

1. Shifts in cultural values are the main causes for changes in the law around the world in relation to animal euthanasia.

   A   B   C

2. Animal testing is cruel and immoral.

   A   B   C

3. Irresponsible owners who do not spay or neuter pets may be the cause of some shelters receiving more surrendered animals than they are capable of re-housing.

   A   B   C

REVIEW YOUR ANSWERS

2. Read the following text before answering the questions as either TRUE, FALSE or CANNOT SAY from the information given.

ANIMAL EUTHANASIA

Animal euthanasia is the practice of terminating the life of an animal in a painless or minimally painful way in order to stop suffering or other undesired conditions in life.

This may be voluntary or involuntary, and carried out with or without a physician. In a medical environment, this can be carried out by oral, intravenous or intramuscular drug administration.1:**Laws around the world vary greatly with regard to animal euthanasia and are constantly subject to change as cultural values shift and better palliative care or treatments become available.** Reasons for animal euthanasia include:

- Terminal illness – eg cancer

- Rabies.

- Behavioural problems (that usually cannot be corrected) – e.g. aggression.

- Illness or broken limbs that would cause suffering for the animal to live with, or when the owner cannot afford (or has a moral objection to) treatment.

- Old age – Deterioration to loss of major bodily functions. Severe impairment of the quality of life.

- Lack of homes – 3: Some shelters receive considerably more surrendered animals than they are capable of re-housing. This may be attributed to irresponsible owners who do not spay or neuter pets, causing unwanted litters. Some pets turned in to animal shelters are not adopted out.

REVIEW YOUR ANSWERS

A – TRUE	B – FALSE	C – CANNOT SAY
Circle A if the question is TRUE from the information provided.	Circle B if the question is FALSE from the information provided.	Circle C if CANNOT SAY from the information provided.

1. Shifts in cultural values are the main causes for changes in the law around the world in relation to animal euthanasia.

A   B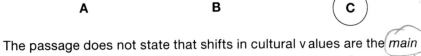

The passage does not state that shifts in cultural values are the *main* causes for changes in the law. Therefore, **we cannot say** from the information provided.

2. Animal testing is cruel and immoral.

A   B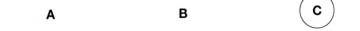

The passage does not provide any information relating to this statement. The correct answer is therefore **cannot say**.

3. Irresponsible owners who do not spay or neuter pets may be the cause of some shelters receiving more surrendered animals than they are capable of re-housing.

                B   C

The passage confirms that this statement is **true**.

3. Read the following text before answering the questions as either TRUE, FALSE or CANNOT SAY from the information given.

WHITEHAM SUPERMARKET

Barry and Bill work at their local supermarket in the town of Whiteham. Barry works every day except Wednesday.

The supermarket is run by Barry's brother Elliot who is married to Sarah. Sarah and Elliot have two children called Marcus and Michelle who are both seven-years-old and they live in the road adjacent to the supermarket.

Barry lives in a town called Redford, which is seven miles from Whiteham. Bill's girlfriend, Maria, works in a factory in her hometown of Brownhaven.

The town of Redford is four miles from Whiteham and six miles from the seaside town of Tenford. Sarah and Elliot take their children on holiday to Tenford twice a year and Barry usually gives them a lift in his car. Barry's mum lives in Tenford and he tries to visit her once a week at 2pm when he is not working.

A – TRUE	**B – FALSE**	**C – CANNOT SAY**
Circle A if the question is TRUE from the information provided.	Circle B if the question is FALSE from the information provided.	Circle C if CANNOT SAY from the information provided.

1. Brownhaven is seven miles from Whiteham.

        A   B   C

2. Barry works at the local supermarket on Sundays.

        A   B   C

3. The town of Redford is four miles from the town of Tenford.

        A   B   C

REVIEW YOUR ANSWERS

3. Read the following text before answering the questions as either TRUE, FALSE or CANNOT SAY from the information given.

WHITEHAM SUPERMARKET

2: Barry and Bill work at their local supermarket in the town of Whiteham. Barry works every day except Wednesday.

The supermarket is run by Barry's brother Elliot who is married to Sarah. Sarah and Elliot have two children called Marcus and Michelle who are both seven-years-old and they live in the road adjacent to the supermarket.

Barry lives in a town called Redford, which is seven miles from Whiteham. Bill's girlfriend, Maria, works in a factory in her hometown of Brownhaven.

3: The town of Redford is four miles from Whiteham and six miles from the seaside town of Tenford. Sarah and Elliot take their children on holiday to Tenford twice a year and Barry usually gives them a lift in his car. Barry's mum lives in Tenford and he tries to visit her once a week at 2pm when he is not working.

REVIEW YOUR ANSWERS

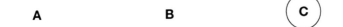

A – TRUE	B – FALSE	C – CANNOT SAY
Circle A if the question is TRUE from the information provided.	Circle B if the question is FALSE from the information provided.	Circle C if CANNOT SAY from the information provided.

1. Brownhaven is seven miles from Whiteham.

A   B   C

Based on the information provided in the passage we **cannot say** whether this statement is true or false.

2. Barry works at the local supermarket on Sundays.

 A   B   C

The passage confirms that *"Barry works every day except Wednesday."* The statement is, therefore, **true**.

3. The town of Redford is four miles from the town of Tenford.

A   B C

The passage states that *"The town of Redford is four miles from Whiteham and six miles from the seaside town of Tenford."* The statement is, therefore, **false** based on the information provided.

4. Read the following text before answering the questions as either TRUE, FALSE or CANNOT SAY from the information given.

NATIONAL INSURANCE CONTRIBUTIONS

People pay National Insurance contributions in order to build up their entitlement to a state pension and other social security benefits.

The amount that you pay is directly linked to the amount you earn. If you earn over a certain amount, your employer deducts Class 1 National Insurance contributions from your wages through the PAYE system.

You pay a lower rate of National Insurance contributions if you're a member of your employer's 'contracted-out' pension scheme, or you're a married woman – or widow – who holds a valid 'election certificate'.

Your employer also pays employer National Insurance contributions based on your earnings and on any benefits you get with your job, for example a company car. HMRC keeps track of your contributions through your National Insurance number. This is like an account number and is unique to you.

A – TRUE	B – FALSE	C – CANNOT SAY
Circle A if the question is TRUE from the information provided.	Circle B if the question is FALSE from the information provided.	Circle C if CANNOT SAY from the information provided.

1. People pay National Insurance contributions in order to build up housing benefits.

     A   B   C

2. HMRC stands for 'Her Majesty's Revenue and Customs'.

     A   B   C

3. An employer pays employer National Insurance contributions if an employee has a company car.

     A   B   C

REVIEW YOUR ANSWERS

4. Read the following text before answering the questions as either TRUE, FALSE or CANNOT SAY from the information given.

NATIONAL INSURANCE CONTRIBUTIONS

1: People pay National Insurance contributions in order to build up their entitlement to a state pension and other social security benefits.

The amount that you pay is directly linked to the amount you earn. If you earn over a certain amount, your employer deducts Class 1 National Insurance contributions from your wages through the PAYE system.

You pay a lower rate of National Insurance contributions if you're a member of your employer's 'contracted-out' pension scheme, or you're a married woman – or widow – who holds a valid 'election certificate'.

3: Your employer also pays employer National Insurance contributions based on your earnings and on any benefits you get with your job, for example a company car. HMRC keeps track of your contributions through your National Insurance number. This is like an account number and is unique to you.

REVIEW YOUR ANSWERS

A – TRUE	B – FALSE	C – CANNOT SAY
Circle A if the question is TRUE from the information provided.	Circle B if the question is FALSE from the information provided.	Circle C if CANNOT SAY from the information provided.

1. People pay National Insurance contributions in order to build up housing benefits.

A   B   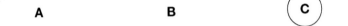 **C**

Although the statement makes reference to social security benefits, it does not confirm these include housing benefits. The correct answer is **cannot say** based on the information provided.

2. HMRC stands for 'Her Majesty's Revenue and Customs'.

A   B   **C**

Yes it does, but the passage makes no reference to this fact; therefore, the correct answer is **cannot say** based on the information provided.

3. An employer pays employer National Insurance contributions if an employee has a company car.

 A   B   C

The passage states that "Your employer also pays employer National Insurance contributions based on your earnings and on any benefits you get with your job, for example a company car". The statement is **true**.

5. Read the following text before answering the questions as either TRUE, FALSE or CANNOT SAY from the information given.

FAMILY HOLIDAY

Janet and Steve have been married for twenty-seven years. They have a daughter called Jessica who is twenty-five-years-old. They all want to go on holiday together but cannot make up their minds where to go.

Janet's first choice would be somewhere hot and sunny abroad. Her second choice would be somewhere in their home country that involves a sporting activity. She does not like hill-climbing or walking holidays but her third choice would be a skiing holiday.

Steve's first choice would be a walking holiday in the hills somewhere in their home country and his second choice would be a sunny holiday abroad. He does not enjoy skiing. Jessica's first choice would be a skiing holiday and her second choice would be a sunny holiday abroad. Jessica's third choice would be a walking holiday in the hills of their home country.

A – TRUE	B – FALSE	C – CANNOT SAY
Circle A if the question is TRUE from the information provided.	Circle B if the question is FALSE from the information provided.	Circle C if CANNOT SAY from the information provided.

1. Jessica's first choice would be a walking holiday in the hills of their home country.

A   B   C

2. Janet and Jessica have been married for twenty-seven years.

A   B   C

3. Jessica would rather go skiing than go on a sunny holiday abroad.

A   B   C

REVIEW YOUR ANSWERS

5. Read the following text before answering the questions as either TRUE, FALSE or CANNOT SAY from the information given.

FAMILY HOLIDAY

2: Janet and Steve have been married for twenty-seven years. They have a daughter called Jessica who is twenty-five-years-old. They all want to go on holiday together but cannot make up their minds where to go.

Janet's first choice would be somewhere hot and sunny abroad. Her second choice would be somewhere in their home country that involves a sporting activity. She does not like hill-climbing or walking holidays but her third choice would be a skiing holiday.

1 & 3: Steve's first choice would be a walking holiday in the hills somewhere in their home country and his second choice would be a sunny holiday abroad. He does not enjoy skiing. Jessica's first choice would be a skiing holiday and her second choice would be a sunny holiday abroad. Jessica's third choice would be a walking holiday in the hills of their home country.

REVIEW YOUR ANSWERS

A – TRUE	**B – FALSE**	**C – CANNOT SAY**
Circle A if the question is TRUE from the information provided.	Circle B if the question is FALSE from the information provided.	Circle C if CANNOT SAY from the information provided.

1. Jessica's first choice would be a walking holiday in the hills of their home country.

A   B C

The passage states that Jessica's first choice would be a skiing holiday; therefore, the sentence is **false**.

2. Janet and Jessica have been married for twenty-seven years.

A   B C

The sentence states that Janet and Jessica have been married, whereas the passage states Janet and Steve. Therefore, the sentence is **false.**

3. Jessica would rather go skiing than go on a sunny holiday abroad.

A   B   C

We can tell from the sentence that Jessica would rather go skiing than go on a sunny holiday abroad as skiing is her first choice. The correct answer is **true**.

Following the five sample questions you should have a better understanding of how the questions are formatted and also how to approach them. You will have gathered that the most important factor when answering the questions is to totally base your answer on the facts that are provided within the passage.

INSIDER TIPS AND ADVICE FOR PASSING VERBAL REASONING TEST

Before you try your first timed test I want to provide you with a number of crucial tips that will give you a better insight into verbal reasoning tests and how you can go about improving your scores.

Tip 1: Don't aim for a set mark, aim to do the best you can

Many people ask me what the scoring criteria are for verbal reasoning tests. They want to know how many they need to get correct in order to pass. To be honest, every employer/test administrator will have a different standard. Tests of this nature in the public sector normally require a pass rate of 70%. My advice would be to not focus on the pass mark but instead focus on trying to get every question correct. Some employers will set the pass mark according to the overall average score amongst the applicants. Therefore, it is pointless worrying about the pass mark.

Tip 2: Practise against the clock

The vast majority of verbal reasoning tests are timed; therefore, you need to practise under timed conditions. Savvy test takers will be fully aware of the amount of time they have to answer each question on average. I encourage you to do the same during your preparation.

Tip 3: Listen to the test administrator

Test administrators should be suitably qualified in order to administer the test. They will provide you with sufficient information on how to take the test and the rules/guidelines involved immediately prior to the real test. This is also your opportunity to ask any questions that you may have. In the majority of cases you will be given the opportunity to try a small number of sample questions.

Tip 4: Don't let the 'odd one out' catch you out

Be prepared to be faced by a variety of test styles. The verbal reasoning test that you are required to undertake should be representative of the type of role you are applying for. That is why you do not see many verbal reasoning tests that require you to 'select the odd one out' or 'fill in the missing words' of a sentence, simply because the majority of occupational roles are not relevant to this type of test. Having said that, the Army still uses a 'select the odd one out' test during its selection process for soldiers.

Tip 5: Keep focused on the test

You should learn to concentrate intently on the test you are taking and the questions you are required to answer. You should learn to block everything that is irrelevant to the test out of your mind. That means not worrying about what the other test takers are doing or where they are in relation to you in the test! Focus on your own test only.

Tip 6: Preparation also includes rest and the right diet

Just about every other psychometric testing book out there will tell you to get some sleep the night before your test. The chances are, you won't be able to rest fully the night before your test. My advice is to get plenty of rest in the fortnight before the test. Eat healthily, get some exercise (brisk walking is perfect) and avoid coffee and alcohol too. I see lots of people drinking energy drinks before their test. Energy drinks may claim to increase stimulation and concentration, but how long for is debatable. The danger is, once the effect wears off, you will start to feel lethargic. Choose clean, healthy water instead.

Tip 7: Obey the test administrator

Test administrators are required to keep a log of events during the test. They are required to write down any incidents that occur, such as noise in neighbouring rooms or interruptions that may occur. They are also required to write down any anomalies that occur with the test takers. Any information that is written down could be used to influence your scores, both good and bad. Follow all instructions carefully and stop writing when told to do so!

Tip 8: Be prepared to say 'cannot say'

As part of your interview skills preparation you're taught to always have something to say in response to a question. You never answer with "don't know" or "can't say", instead you always seek to find a relevant response which will put you in a good light. So for many test takers it is unnerving to answer with the option 'cannot say'. In fact this is often the reason some companies use this specific abbreviation – to test your nerve. So it is important to remember that 'cannot say' is only an abbreviation of the 'cannot say on the information provided' option and is a valid answer from observant and successful candidates.

The next element of your preparation is to include 'time'. I am now going to provide you with your first timed test. The test that follows consists of ten sample tests and you have ten minutes in which to complete them. You will note that you have an average of sixty seconds per question. As per my previous advice, if you find that you are spending well over the average time allocation on a particular question, you should move on to the next one.

If you complete the test within the allotted time, go back over any questions you were unsure of and thoroughly check them.

Please use a pencil to circle your chosen answers. I also recommend that you have a stopwatch or clock with you so that you can keep a check on the time.

When you are ready, turn the page and begin. The answers and explanations are provided at the end of the test.

TEST 1
VERBAL
REASONING

During Verbal Reasoning Test 1 there are 10 practice passages which each contain 3 questions. Answer each question based solely on the information provided. You must select either TRUE, FALSE or CANNOT SAY based on the information provided in the passage.

- You have 10 minutes to complete the test.
- Concentrate fully on each test.
- Circle the answer you believe to be correct.
- If unsure of an answer you should select the one that you believe to be correct.
- Avoid all forms of wild guessing.

Once you have completed the test check your answers with the ones that are provided.

1. Read the following text before answering the questions as either TRUE, FALSE or CANNOT SAY from the information given.

ANALYSTS PROVE FORECASTERS WRONG

The Office for National Statistics said internet shopping and sales of household goods had been better in October compared with previous months. However, sales of clothing and footwear, where many retailers cut prices before Christmas, were particularly weak.

The increase came as a surprise to many analysts who were predicting a 0.4% fall in internet shopping and sales of household goods. The rise meant that retail sales volumes in the three months to January were up by 2.6% on the previous quarter. The final quarter of the year is a better guide to the underlying trend than one month's figures.

Some analysts cautioned that the heavy seasonal adjustment of the raw spending figures at the turn of the year made interpreting the data difficult. Even so, the government will be relieved that spending appears to be holding up despite the squeeze on incomes caused by high inflation, rising unemployment, a weak housing market and the crisis in the eurozone.

Retail sales account for less than half of total consumer spending and do not include the purchase of cars or eating out. The ONS said that its measure of inflation in the high street – the annual retail sales deflator – fell to 2.2% last month, its lowest level since November 2009. Ministers are hoping that lower inflation will boost real income growth during the course of 2012.

A – TRUE	B – FALSE	C – CANNOT SAY
Circle A if the question is TRUE from the information provided.	Circle B if the question is FALSE from the information provided.	Circle C if CANNOT SAY from the information provided.

1. Ministers hope that higher inflation will boost real income growth during 2012.

A   B   C

2. Analyst's predicted a 0.4% rise in the sales of household goods.

A   B   C

3. The crisis in the eurozone is contributing to the squeeze on incomes.

A   B   C

2. Read the following text before answering the questions as either TRUE, FALSE or CANNOT SAY from the information given.

LONG-SERVICE PAYMENTS

Employees who attain fifteen years' continuous service between 7th November 2003 and 30th June 2007 shall qualify for the long-service payment at the rate applicable at the time. Employees who are promoted to a higher role during this period will cease to qualify for the payment but will receive a minimum pay increase on promotion of £300 per annum, which will be achieved through partial protection of the long-service payment.

Where the pay assimilation process on 7th November 2003 created a basic pay increase of more than 7%, and the employee was in receipt of the long-service payment, the payment has been reduced with effect from that date by the amount that the increase exceeded 7%. The consequent pay rates were set out in circular NJC/01/04.

PAY PROTECTION FOR EMPLOYEES ON THE RETAINED DUTY SYSTEM

Where an employee on the retained duty system has not received a pay increase of at least 7% (for the same pattern and level of activity) following full implementation of the pay award effective from 7th November 2003, the fire and rescue authority may introduce arrangements to ensure that such an increase is achieved.

ACTING UP AND TEMPORARY PROMOTION

The NJC recognises that in the early stages of implementing the Integrated Personal Development System it may, on occasions, be difficult to apply the principles at Paragraph 19 of Section 4 Part B. Fire and rescue authorities, employees and trade unions should therefore adopt a co-operative and common sense approach to any problems that might arise.

A – TRUE	**B – FALSE**	**C – CANNOT SAY**
Circle A if the question is TRUE from the information provided.	Circle B if the question is FALSE from the information provided.	Circle C if CANNOT SAY from the information provided.

1. If an employee who is on the retained duty system has not received a pay increase of at least 7% following the introduction of the pay award, the fire and rescue service must introduce arrangements to ensure that such an increase is achieved.

    A   B   C

2. Employees who attain fifteen years' continuous service between 7th November 2003 and 30th June 2008 shall qualify for the long-service payment at the rate applicable at the time.

    A   B   C

3. The pay assimilation process on 7th November 2003 created a basic pay increase for all employees of more than 7%.

    A   B   C

3. Read the following text before answering the questions as either TRUE, FALSE or CANNOT SAY from the information given.

DATA WAREHOUSES

A data warehouse is the main source of information for an organisation's historical data. Its historical data is often referred to as its corporate memory. As an example of how a data warehouse can be put to good use, an organisation would use the information stored in its data warehouse to find out how many particular stock items they sold on a particular day in a particular year. They could also ascertain which employees were off sick on any given day or any given year. The data stored within the warehouse contains essential information so that managers can make appropriate management decisions.

A data warehouse is normally large in size as the information stored usually focuses on basic, structured and organised data. Some of the characteristics of the data in a data warehouse are as follows:

Time-variant - changes to the data in the database are tracked and recorded so that reports can be produced showing changes over time;

Non-volatile - the data in the database is never over-written or deleted but is retained for future reporting;

Integrated - the database contains data from most or all of an organisation's operational applications and this data is useful and meaningful for further processing and analysis.

A – TRUE	B – FALSE	C – CANNOT SAY
Circle A if the question is TRUE from the information provided.	Circle B if the question is FALSE from the information provided.	Circle C if CANNOT SAY from the information provided.

1. Integrated and non-volatile data form some of the characteristics of a data warehouse.

 A   **B**   **C**

2. It is not possible to identify which employees were on sick leave from the information stored in a data warehouse.

A   **B**   **C**

3. Corporate memory is an alternative name given to historical data.

A   **B**   **C**

4. Read the following text before answering the questions as either TRUE, FALSE or CANNOT SAY from the information given.

THE IMPORTANCE OF HEALTH AND SAFETY IN THE WORKPLACE

You must protect the safety and health of everyone in your workplace, including people with disabilities, and provide welfare facilities for your employees.

Basic things you need to consider are outlined below.

WELFARE FACILITIES

For your employees' well-being you need to provide:

- toilets and hand basins, with soap and towels or a hand-dryer; drinking water.
- a place to store clothing (and somewhere to change if special clothing is worn for work).
- somewhere to rest and eat meals.

HEALTH ISSUES

To have a healthy working environment, make sure there is:

- good ventilation – a supply of fresh, clean air drawn from outside or a ventilation system.
- a reasonable working temperature (usually at least 16°C, or 13°C for strenuous work, unless other laws require lower temperatures).
- lighting suitable for the work being carried out.
- enough room space and suitable workstations and seating.
- a clean workplace with appropriate waste containers.

SAFETY ISSUES

To keep your workplace safe you must:

- properly maintain your premises and work equipment.
- keep floors and traffic routes free from obstruction.
- have windows that can be opened and also cleaned safely.
- make sure that any transparent (eg glass) doors or walls are protected or made of safety material.

A – TRUE	B – FALSE	C – CANNOT SAY
Circle A if the question is TRUE from the information provided.	Circle B if the question is FALSE from the information provided.	Circle C if CANNOT SAY from the information provided.

1. It is the responsibility of the employee for keeping a workplace safe.

    A   B   C

2. Providing the employee with a suitable workstation is a consideration for the employer when making the workplace safe.

    A   B   C

3. An employer must ensure that all floor surfaces are non-slip in order to prevent slips, trips and falls.

    A   B   C

5. Read the following text before answering the questions as either TRUE, FALSE or CANNOT SAY from the information given.

MAGISTRATE TRAINING

The entire selection process for becoming a magistrate can take approximately 12 months, sometimes longer depending on the area.

Once you have been accepted you will be required to undertake a comprehensive training course which is usually held over a 3-day period (18 hours). During this course you will learn the necessary skills that are required in order to become a magistrate.

The training is normally carried out by the Justice Clerk who is responsible for the court. He/she will usually be the legal advisor during your magistrate sittings. They will help you to develop all the necessary skills required in order to carry out your duties professionally and competently.

You will carry out your training as part of a group with other people who have been recruited at the same time as you. This is extremely beneficial as it will allow you to learn in a safe environment.

Training will be given using a variety of methods, which may include pre-course reading, small-group work, use of case studies, computer-based training and CCTV. It is recognised that magistrates are volunteers and that their time is valuable, so every effort is made to provide all training at times and places convenient to trainees. The Ministry of Justice booklet 'Serving as a Magistrate' has more information about the magistracy and the role of magistrates.

A – TRUE	**B – FALSE**	**C – CANNOT SAY**
Circle A if the question is TRUE from the information provided.	Circle B if the question is FALSE from the information provided.	Circle C if CANNOT SAY from the information provided.

1. The comprehensive training course for becoming a magistrate usually consists of 3 days which is divided into 6 hours training per day.

   A   B   C

2. An applicant can find out more about the role of a magistrate by reading the Ministry of Justice booklet 'Serving as a Magistrate'.

   A   B   C

3. The selection process for becoming a magistrate will take no longer than 12 months.

   A   B   C

6. Read the following text before answering the questions as either TRUE, FALSE or CANNOT SAY from the information given.

HOW TO ENROL IN OUR ONLINE SELLERS' PROGRAMME

To enrol in our online sellers' programme, you must have an email account, access to the Internet, have a UK distribution facility and also hold the full UK distribution rights to the item(s) you want to sell.

You must have a UK bank account capable of receiving payments via electronic bank transfer (BACS), as this is the only method of payment we offer. Each product you wish to sell in our programme must meet our minimum eligibility standards. These standards relate to quality, value, subject matter, production standards and compliance with intellectual property laws. We reserve the right to remove any products if they do not meet our standards. You are not permitted to sell any products that are deemed to be pornographic or racist.

Any books that you wish to sell via our sellers' programme must have a 10 or 13 digit ISBN number and applicable barcode printed on the back of the book in the bottom right-hand corner.

The barcode must scan to match the ISBN of the book. If the item you want to sell is a music CD then the CD must be in a protective case which meets the relevant British Standard.

The title and artist name must be printed on and readable from the spine (the thin side of the CD). Once again, the CD must contain a barcode which must scan to match the EAN or UPC.

If your item is a DVD or VHS video. Rules that apply to music CDs are also applicable to DVD products.

A – TRUE	B – FALSE	C – CANNOT SAY
Circle A if the question is TRUE from the information provided.	Circle B if the question is FALSE from the information provided.	Circle C if CANNOT SAY from the information provided.

1. The barcode on a CD must be printed on back in the bottom right-hand corner

   A   B   C

2. Pornographic products are permitted in the online sellers' programme.

   A   B   C

3. ISBN is short for International Standard Book Number.

   A   B   C

7. Read the following text before answering the questions as either TRUE, FALSE or CANNOT SAY from the information given.

WHAT CRITERIA DO WE USE TO DECIDE IF TRADE DISTRIBUTION IS APPROPRIATE?

Firstly, we will only consider a distribution relationship with publishers who have a UK-based storage and representation arrangement. Generally we will hold a larger stock than would normally be required of a wholesaler, but we do need to have easy access to top-up facilities within the UK.

In addition, it is imperative that the titles are represented to the trade in order to generate UK sales. Whether this is via a UK-based sales/marketing presence, or one based overseas, is not important, as long as it is effective in selling the titles to the target audience. Although we offer some promotional assistance through our weekly/monthly publications we do not offer sales and marketing as a service per se.

MINIMUM TURNOVER/LINES

The publisher should normally be able to demonstrate a realistic expectation of turnover in excess of £50k per annum at RRP and have a minimum of 5 lines. However, these targets are both negotiable where appropriate.

WHAT TERMS WILL BE REQUIRED?

Final discount and credit terms will be agreed on a case-by-case basis. Stock will be held on a consignment basis and we will provide monthly statements of sales and other management information. Invoicing will be against sales achieved each month and within the credit terms agreed.

A –TRUE	B – FALSE	C – CANNOT SAY
Circle A if the question is TRUE from the information provided.	Circle B if the question is FALSE from the information provided.	Circle C if CANNOT SAY from the information provided.

1. All invoices are paid 30 days in arrears.

        A   B   C

2. An application from a publisher with a turnover of £49k will not be accepted.

        A   B   C

3. Applicants who reside in southern Ireland will not be considered for a trade account.

        A   B   C

8. Read the following text before answering the questions as either TRUE, FALSE or CANNOT SAY from the information given.

THE ROLE OF THE AMBULANCE SERVICE

Most people believe that the Ambulance Service is simply there to respond to emergency incidents such as road traffic collisions (RTCs), seriously ill or injured patients, fires and other such incidents. While these are the core roles that the service undertakes, there are also a number of other important duties that are carried out, such as patient transport services.

The latter is carried out by the employees of the Ambulance Service who carry disabled, elderly and vulnerable people to and from out-patient appointments, hospital admissions and also day centres and clinics. Behind the operational ambulance crew is a team of people who have different roles, all designed to provide the necessary support required that is so valued by the community.

To begin with, there are the 999 call operators who take the initial calls. Their job is to gather as much information as possible about the emergency call, the nature of the incident, its location and the level of response that is required.

These people are integral to the Ambulance Service and are crucial to patient care. For example, if a patient is critically ill they may need to talk the caller through a life-saving procedure while they wait for the ambulance crews to get there.

A – TRUE	B – FALSE	C – CANNOT SAY
Circle A if the question is TRUE from the information provided.	Circle B if the question is FALSE from the information provided.	Circle C if CANNOT SAY from the information provided.

1. The 999 call operators do not travel in the ambulance with the paramedics.

$$A \qquad\qquad B \qquad\qquad C$$

2. Responding to road traffic collisions forms part of the core role of the Ambulance Service.

$$A \qquad\qquad B \qquad\qquad C$$

3. 999 call operators may need to talk the caller through a life-saving procedure while they wait for the ambulance crews to get there.

$$A \qquad\qquad B \qquad\qquad C$$

9. Read the following text before answering the questions as either TRUE, FALSE or CANNOT SAY from the information given.

WHAT IS A CUSTOMER CHARTER?

A Customer Charter is a statement as to how a company will deliver a quality customer service. The main purpose of a Customer Charter is to inform customers of the standards of service to expect, what to do if something goes wrong and how to make a complaint. In addition to this a Customer Charter also helps employees by setting out clearly defined standards of how they should perform within the organisation in relation to customer service delivery.

IS IT NECESSARY FOR AN ORGANISATION TO HAVE ONE?

Whilst not a legal requirement, a Customer Charter is an ideal way of helping organisations define with their customers, and others, what that service should be and the standard that should be expected. The charter will also help customers get the most from an organisation's services, including how to make a complaint if they are dissatisfied with any aspect of service or if they have ideas for improvement.

OTHER POINTS TO CONSIDER

A Customer Charter should be written in a clear and user-friendly manner. In addition to this, a Crystal Mark endorsement by the Plain English Campaign would enhance its status. If appropriate, it should be displayed in a prominent place, so all customers can see it. The Customer Charter must be available in different formats, such as large print and audio, so that customers with particular needs can access it. If an organisation is part of an industry where a regulator has been appointed, details of how to contact the regulator should be included.

A –TRUE	B – FALSE	C – CANNOT SAY
Circle A if the question is TRUE from the information provided.	Circle B if the question is FALSE from the information provided.	Circle C if CANNOT SAY from the information provided.

1. A Customer Charter is a legal requirement within an organisation.

        A   B   C

2. A Customer Charter must be written using a Crystal Mark endorsement by the Plain English Campaign.

        A   B   C

3. The Customer Charter may be available in different formats, such as large print and audio, so that customers with particular needs can access it.

        A   B   C

10. Read the following text before answering the questions as either TRUE, FALSE or CANNOT SAY from the information given.

WHAT IS A BALANCE SHEET?

A balance sheet is a snapshot of a company's financial position at a particular point of time in contrast to an income statement, which measures income over a period of time.

A balance sheet is usually calculated for March 31, last day of the financial year. A financial year starts on April 1 and ends on March 31. For example, the period between April 1, 2011 and March 31, 2012 will complete a financial year. A balance sheet measures three kinds of variables: assets, liabilities and shareholder's equity.

Assets are things like factories and machinery that the company uses to create value for its customers. Liabilities are what the company owes to third parties (eg outstanding payments to suppliers). Equity is the money initially invested by shareholders plus the retained earnings over the years. These three variables are linked by the relationship: Assets = Liabilities + Shareholder's equity. Both assets and liabilities are further classified based on their liquidity, that is, how easily they can be converted into cash.

Current liabilities are liabilities that are due within a year and include interest payments, dividend payments and accounts payable. Long-term assets include fixed assets like land and factories as well as intangible assets like goodwill and brands. Finally, long-term liabilities are basically debt with maturity of more than a year.

A – TRUE	**B – FALSE**	**C – CANNOT SAY**
Circle A if the question is TRUE from the information provided.	Circle B if the question is FALSE from the information provided.	Circle C if CANNOT SAY from the information provided.

1. A financial year starts on March 31 and ends on April 1.

A   B   C

2. It can be said that the liquidity of both assets and liabilities is how easily they can be converted into cash.

A   B   C

3. A balance sheet is a legal requirement and every company must have one.

A   B   C

Now that you have reached the end of the test, check your answers with the ones that are provided in the next section.

ANSWERS AND EXPLANATIONS TO VERBAL REASONING TEST 1

1. Read the following text before answering the questions as either TRUE, FALSE or CANNOT SAY from the information given.

ANALYSTS PROVE FORECASTERS WRONG

The Office for National Statistics said internet shopping and sales of household goods had been better in October compared with previous months. However, sales of clothing and footwear, where many retailers cut prices before Christmas, were particularly weak.

2: The increase came as a surprise to many analysts who were predicting a 0.4% fall in internet shopping and sales of household goods. The rise meant that retail sales volumes in the three months to January were up by 2.6% on the previous quarter. The final quarter of the year is a better guide to the underlying trend than one month's figures.

Some analysts cautioned that the heavy seasonal adjustment of the raw spending figures at the turn of the year made interpreting the data difficult. Even so, the government will be relieved that spending appears to be holding up **3: despite the squeeze on incomes caused by high inflation, rising unemployment, a weak housing market and the crisis in the eurozone.**

Retail sales account for less than half of total consumer spending and do not include the purchase of cars or eating out. The ONS said that its measure of inflation in the high street – the annual retail sales deflator – fell to 2.2% last month, its lowest level since November 2009. **1: Ministers are hoping that lower inflation will boost real income growth during the course of 2012.**

A – TRUE	B – FALSE	C – CANNOT SAY
Circle A if the question is TRUE from the information provided.	Circle B if the question is FALSE from the information provided.	Circle C if CANNOT SAY from the information provided.

1. Ministers hope that higher inflation will boost real income growth during 2012.

The sentence states that ministers hope that 'lower' inflation will boost real income growth, not higher. Therefore, the statement is **false**.

2. Analyst's predicted a 0.4% rise in the sales of household goods.

The passage states that analysts were predicting a 0.4% fall in sales of household goods, not rise. Therefore, the statement is **false**.

3. The crisis in the eurozone is contributing to the squeeze on incomes.

A   B   C

This statement is **true** based on the information provided in the passage.

2. Read the following text before answering the questions as either TRUE, FALSE or CANNOT SAY from the information given.

LONG-SERVICE PAYMENTS

2: Employees who attain fifteen years' continuous service between 7th November 2003 and 30th June 2007 shall qualify for the long-service payment at the rate applicable at the time. Employees who are promoted to a higher role during this period will cease to qualify for the payment but will receive a minimum pay increase on promotion of £300 per annum, which will be achieved through partial protection of the long-service payment.

Where the pay assimilation process on 7th November 2003 created a basic pay increase of more than 7%, and the employee was in receipt of the long-service payment, the payment has been reduced with effect from that date by the amount that the increase exceeded 7%. The consequent pay rates were set out in circular NJC/01/04.

PAY PROTECTION FOR EMPLOYEES ON THE RETAINED DUTY SYSTEM

1: Where an employee on the retained duty system has not received a pay increase of at least 7% (for the same pattern and level of activity) following full implementation of the pay award effective from 7th November 2003, the fire and rescue authority may introduce arrangements to ensure that such an increase is achieved.

ACTING UP AND TEMPORARY PROMOTION

The NJC recognises that in the early stages of implementing the Integrated Personal Development System it may, on occasions, be difficult to apply the principles at Paragraph 19 of Section 4 Part B. Fire and rescue authorities, employees and trade unions should therefore adopt a co-operative and common sense approach to any problems that might arise.

A – TRUE	**B – FALSE**	**C – CANNOT SAY**
Circle A if the question is TRUE from the information provided.	Circle B if the question is FALSE from the information provided.	Circle C if CANNOT SAY from the information provided.

1. If an employee who is on the retained duty system has not received a pay increase of at least 7% following the introduction of the pay award, the fire and rescue service must introduce arrangements to ensure that such an increase is achieved.

A   B   C

This statement is **false** because the sentence states that the fire and rescue service 'may' introduce arrangements; it does not say they 'must'.

2. Employees who attain fifteen years' continuous service between 7th November 2003 and 30th June 2008 shall qualify for the long-service payment at the rate applicable at the time.

A   B   C

This statement is **false** because the sentence states 30th June 2008, instead of 30th June 2007 as stated in the passage.

3. The pay assimilation process on 7th November 2003 created a basic pay increase for all employees of more than 7%.

A   B   C

We **cannot say** that this statement is true or false. It makes no reference in the passage that 'all' employees received a pay rise.

3. Read the following text before answering the questions as either TRUE, FALSE or CANNOT SAY from the information given.

DATA WAREHOUSES

A data warehouse is the main source of information for an organisation's historical data. **3: Its historical data is often referred to as its corporate memory.** As an example of how a data warehouse can be put to good use, an organisation would use the information stored in its data warehouse to find out how many particular stock items they sold on a particular day in a particular year. **2: They could also ascertain which employees were off sick on any given day or any given year.** The data stored within the warehouse contains essential information so that managers can make appropriate management decisions.

A data warehouse is normally large in size as the information stored usually focuses on basic, structured and organised data. **1: Some of the characteristics of the data in a data warehouse are as follows:**

Time-variant - changes to the data in the database are tracked and recorded so that reports can be produced showing changes over time;

Non-volatile - the data in the database is never over-written or deleted but is retained for future reporting;

Integrated - the database contains data from most or all of an organisation's operational applications and this data is useful and meaningful for further processing and analysis.

A – TRUE	B – FALSE	C – CANNOT SAY
Circle A if the question is TRUE from the information provided.	Circle B if the question is FALSE from the information provided.	Circle C if CANNOT SAY from the information provided.

1. Integrated and non-volatile data form some of the characteristics of a data warehouse.

  B C

It is **true**, according to the passage, that some of the characteristics of a data warehouse include integrated and non-volatile data.

2. It is not possible to identify which employees were on sick leave from the information stored in a data warehouse.

A  C

It is possible to ascertain which employees were off sick from the information stored in a data warehouse; therefore, the statement is **false**.

3. Corporate memory is an alternative name given to historical data.

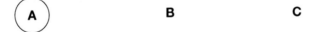 B C

It is **true** that corporate memory is an alternative name given to historical data.

4. Read the following text before answering the questions as either TRUE, FALSE or CANNOT SAY from the information given.

THE IMPORTANCE OF HEALTH AND SAFETY IN THE WORKPLACE

You must protect the safety and health of everyone in your workplace, including people with disabilities, and provide welfare facilities for your employees.

Basic things you need to consider are outlined below.

WELFARE FACILITIES

For your employees' well-being you need to provide:

- toilets and hand basins, with soap and towels or a hand-dryer, drinking water.
- a place to store clothing (and somewhere to change if special clothing is worn for work).
- somewhere to rest and eat meals.

HEALTH ISSUES

To have a healthy working environment, make sure there is:

- good ventilation – a supply of fresh, clean air drawn from outside or a ventilation system.
- a reasonable working temperature (usually at least 16°C, or 13°C for strenuous work, unless other laws require lower temperatures).
- lighting suitable for the work being carried out.
- **2: enough room space and suitable workstations and seating.**
- a clean workplace with appropriate waste containers.

SAFETY ISSUES

To keep your workplace safe you must:

- properly maintain your premises and work equipment.
- keep floors and traffic routes free from obstruction.
- have windows that can be opened and also cleaned safely.
- make sure that any transparent (eg glass) doors or walls are protected or made of safety material.

A – TRUE	**B – FALSE**	**C – CANNOT SAY**
Circle A if the question is TRUE from the information provided.	Circle B if the question is FALSE from the information provided.	Circle C if CANNOT SAY from the information provided.

1. It is the responsibility of the employee for keeping a workplace safe.

A   B   C

The passage makes no reference to this statement. Therefore, we cannot say whether the statement is true or false from the information provided. **Cannot say** is the correct answer.

2. Providing the employee with a suitable workstation is a consideration for the employer when making the workplace safe.

A   B   C

We can deduce from the passage that this statement is **true**.

3. An employer must ensure that all floor surfaces are non-slip in order to prevent slips, trips and falls.

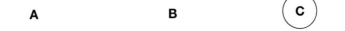

A   B   C

In health and safety law this statement is true. However, the passage makes no reference it. **Cannot say** is the correct answer.

5. Read the following text before answering the questions as either TRUE, FALSE or CANNOT SAY from the information given.

MAGISTRATE TRAINING

3: The entire selection process for becoming a magistrate can take approximately 12 months, sometimes longer depending on the area.

1: Once you have been accepted you will be required to undertake a comprehensive training course which is usually held over a 3-day period (18 hours). During this course you will learn the necessary skills that are required in order to become a magistrate.

The training is normally carried out by the Justice Clerk who is responsible for the court. He/she will usually be the legal advisor during your magistrate sittings. They will help you to develop all the necessary skills required in order to carry out your duties professionally and competently.

You will carry out your training as part of a group with other people who have been recruited at the same time as you. This is extremely beneficial as it will allow you to learn in a safe environment.

Training will be given using a variety of methods, which may include pre-course reading, small-group work, use of case studies, computer-based training and CCTV. It is recognised that magistrates are volunteers and that their time is valuable, so every effort is made to provide all training at times and places convenient to trainees. 2: The Ministry of Justice booklet 'Serving as a Magistrate' has more information about the magistracy and the role of magistrates.

A – TRUE	B – FALSE	C – CANNOT SAY
Circle A if the question is TRUE from the information provided.	Circle B if the question is FALSE from the information provided.	Circle C if CANNOT SAY from the information provided.

1. The comprehensive training course for becoming a magistrate usually consists of 3 days which is divided into 6 hours training per day.

A   B   C

The passage does state that the training course is usually held over a 3-day period (18 hours). We could assume that the 18 hours are equally divided into 3 x 6 hour days. However, it is not our job to assume; we must base our answers on what is provided within the passage. Therefore, the correct answer is **cannot say**.

2. An applicant can find out more about the role of a magistrate by reading the Ministry of Justice booklet 'Serving as a Magistrate'.

A   B   C

From the passage we know this statement to be **true.**

3. The selection process for becoming a magistrate will take no longer than 12 months.

A    B C

This statement is **false** because the passage states that the selection process can sometimes take longer than 12 months.

6. Read the following text before answering the questions as either TRUE, FALSE or CANNOT SAY from the information given.

HOW TO ENROL IN OUR ONLINE SELLERS' PROGRAMME

To enrol in our online sellers' programme, you must have an email account, access to the Internet, have a UK distribution facility and also hold the full UK distribution rights to the item(s) you want to sell.

You must have a UK bank account capable of receiving payments via electronic bank transfer (BACS), as this is the only method of payment we offer. Each product you wish to sell in our programme must meet our minimum eligibility standards. These standards relate to quality, value, subject matter, production standards and compliance with intellectual property laws. We reserve the right to remove any products if they do not meet our standards. **2: You are not permitted to sell any products that are deemed to be pornographic or racist.**

Any books that you wish to sell via our sellers' programme must have a 10 or 13 digit ISBN number and applicable barcode printed on the back of the book in the bottom right-hand corner.

The barcode must scan to match the ISBN of the book. If the item you want to sell is a music CD then the CD must be in a protective case which meets the relevant British Standard.

The title and artist name must be printed on and readable from the spine (the thin side of the CD). **1: Once again, the CD must contain a barcode which must scan to match the EAN or UPC.**

If your item is a DVD or VHS video. Rules that apply to music CDs are also applicable to DVD products.

A – TRUE	B – FALSE	C – CANNOT SAY
Circle A if the question is TRUE from the information provided.	Circle B if the question is FALSE from the information provided.	Circle C if CANNOT SAY from the information provided.

1. The barcode on a CD must be printed on back in the bottom right-hand corner

A   B   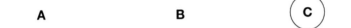C

The passage does state that a CD will require a barcode. However, unlike the reference to the location of the barcode on books, it makes no reference to the barcode location for CDs. Therefore the answer is **cannot say**.

2. Pornographic products are permitted in the online sellers' programme.

A   B C

The passage clearly states that pornographic products are not permitted. Therefore, the correct answer is **false**.

3. ISBN is short for International Standard Book Number.

A   B   C

This statement is true. However, the passage makes no reference to it. The correct answer is **cannot say** based on the information provided.

7. Read the following text before answering the questions as either TRUE, FALSE or CANNOT SAY from the information given.

WHAT CRITERIA DO WE USE TO DECIDE IF TRADE DISTRIBUTION IS APPROPRIATE?

3: Firstly, we will only consider a distribution relationship with publishers who have a UK-based storage and representation arrangement. Generally we will hold a larger stock than would normally be required of a wholesaler, but we do need to have easy access to top-up facilities within the UK.

In addition, it is imperative that the titles are represented to the trade in order to generate UK sales. Whether this is via a UK-based sales/marketing presence, or one based overseas, is not important, as long as it is effective in selling the titles to the target audience. Although we offer some promotional assistance through our weekly/monthly publications we do not offer sales and marketing as a service per se.

MINIMUM TURNOVER/LINES

2: The publisher should normally be able to demonstrate a realistic expectation of turnover in excess of £50k per annum at RRP and have a minimum of 5 lines. However, these targets are both negotiable where appropriate.

WHAT TERMS WILL BE REQUIRED?

Final discount and credit terms will be agreed on a case-by-case basis. Stock will be held on a consignment basis and we will provide monthly statements of sales and other management information. **1: Invoicing will be against sales achieved each month and within the credit terms agreed.**

A – TRUE	**B – FALSE**	**C – CANNOT SAY**
Circle A if the question is TRUE from the information provided.	Circle B if the question is FALSE from the information provided.	Circle C if CANNOT SAY from the information provided.

1. All invoices are paid 30 days in arrears.

A   B   **C**

The passage makes no reference to this statement. The answer is **cannot say** from the information provided.

2. An application from a publisher with a turnover of £49k will not be accepted.

A   B   **C**

Although the passage makes reference to an expected turnover of £50k per annum, it also states that the targets are negotiable. Because the targets are negotiable, we cannot confirm whether the statement is true or false. As such, we must select **cannot say** as the correct answer.

3. Applicants who reside in southern Ireland will not be considered for a trade account.

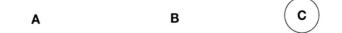

A   B   **C**

The passage states that they will only consider a distribution relationship with publishers who have a UK-based storage and representation arrangement. Southern Ireland does not form part of the UK. However, the statement doesn't makes reference to applicants who 'reside' in southern Ireland. Because an applicant resides in southern Ireland we cannot say whether or not their application will be considered, simply because there is nothing to prevent a resident of southern Ireland from having a UK-based storage and representation arrangement. Therefore, the correct answer is **cannot say** from the information provided.

8. Read the following text before answering the questions as either TRUE, FALSE or CANNOT SAY from the information given.

THE ROLE OF THE AMBULANCE SERVICE

Most people believe that the Ambulance Service is simply there to respond to emergency incidents such as 2: road traffic collisions (RTCs), seriously ill or injured patients, fires and other such incidents. While these are the core roles that the service undertakes, there are also a number of other important duties that are carried out, such as patient transport services.

The latter is carried out by the employees of the Ambulance Service who carry disabled, elderly and vulnerable people to and from out-patient appointments, hospital admissions and also day centres and clinics. Behind the operational ambulance crew is a team of people who have different roles, all designed to provide the necessary support required that is so valued by the community.

To begin with, there are the 999 call operators who take the initial calls. Their job is to gather as much information as possible about the emergency call, the nature of the incident, its location and the level of response that is required.

These people are integral to the Ambulance Service and are crucial to patient care. For example, 3: if a patient is critically ill they may need to talk the caller through a life-saving procedure while they wait for the ambulance crews to get there.

A – TRUE	B – FALSE	C – CANNOT SAY
Circle A if the question is TRUE from the information provided.	Circle B if the question is FALSE from the information provided.	Circle C if CANNOT SAY from the information provided.

1. The 999 call operators do not travel in the ambulance with the paramedics.

    A   B   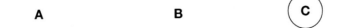 C

The passage makes no reference to this statement. The correct answer is **cannot say** from the information provided.

2. Responding to road traffic collisions forms part of the core role of the Ambulance Service.

     A   B   C

The passage makes it clear that responding to road traffic collisions is a core role for the Ambulance Service. The statement is **true**.

3. 999 call operators may need to talk the caller through a life-saving procedure while they wait for the ambulance crews to get there.

     A   B   C

From the passage we can confirm that this statement is **true**.

9. Read the following text before answering the questions as either TRUE, FALSE or CANNOT SAY from the information given.

WHAT IS A CUSTOMER CHARTER?

A Customer Charter is a statement as to how a company will deliver a quality customer service. The main purpose of a Customer Charter is to inform customers of the standards of service to expect, what to do if something goes wrong and how to make a complaint. In addition to this a Customer Charter also helps employees by setting out clearly defined standards of how they should perform within the organisation in relation to customer service delivery.

IS IT NECESSARY FOR AN ORGANISATION TO HAVE ONE?

1: Whilst not a legal requirement, a Customer Charter is an ideal way of helping organisations define with their customers, and others, what that service should be and the standard that should be expected. The charter will also help customers get the most from an organisation's services, including how to make a complaint if they are dissatisfied with any aspect of service or if they have ideas for improvement.

OTHER POINTS TO CONSIDER

2: A Customer Charter should be written in a clear and user-friendly manner. In addition to this, a Crystal Mark endorsement by the Plain English Campaign would enhance its status. If appropriate, it should be displayed in a prominent place, so all customers can see it. 3: The Customer Charter must be available in different formats, such as large print and audio, so that customers with particular needs can access it. If an organisation is part of an industry where a regulator has been appointed, details of how to contact the regulator should be included.

A – TRUE	B – FALSE	C – CANNOT SAY
Circle A if the question is TRUE from the information provided.	Circle B if the question is FALSE from the information provided.	Circle C if CANNOT SAY from the information provided.

1. A Customer Charter is a legal requirement within an organisation.

A  C

The passage clearly states that a Customer Charter is not a legal requirement. The correct answer is **false**.

2. A Customer Charter must be written using a Crystal Mark endorsement by the Plain English Campaign.

A  C

The passage states that a Customer Charter should be written in a clear and user-friendly manner. It states that a Crystal Mark endorsement by the Plain English Campaign would enhance its status. However the use of a Crystal Mark is not compulsory. Therefore, the statement is **false.**

3. The Customer Charter may be available in different formats, such as large print and audio, so that customers with particular needs can access it.

A C

The passage states that "The Customer Charter must be available…"
The statement above states that it 'may' be available. Therefore, it is **false**.

10. Read the following text before answering the questions as either TRUE, FALSE or CANNOT SAY from the information given.

WHAT IS A BALANCE SHEET?

A balance sheet is a snapshot of a company's financial position at a particular point of time in contrast to an income statement, which measures income over a period of time.

A balance sheet is usually calculated for March 31, last day of the financial year. **1: A financial year starts on April 1 and ends on March 31.** For example, the period between April 1, 2011 and March 31, 2012 will complete a financial year. A balance sheet measures three kinds of variables: assets, liabilities and shareholder's equity.

Assets are things like factories and machinery that the company uses to create value for its customers. Liabilities are what the company owes to third parties (eg outstanding payments to suppliers). Equity is the money initially invested by shareholders plus the retained earnings over the years. These three variables are linked by the relationship: Assets = Liabilities + Shareholder's equity. **2: Both assets and liabilities are further classified based on their liquidity, that is, how easily they can be converted into cash.**

Current liabilities are liabilities that are due within a year and include interest payments, dividend payments and accounts payable. Long-term assets include fixed assets like land and factories as well as intangible assets like goodwill and brands. Finally, long-term liabilities are basically debt with maturity of more than a year.

A – TRUE	**B – FALSE**	**C – CANNOT SAY**
Circle A if the question is TRUE from the information provided.	Circle B if the question is FALSE from the information provided.	Circle C if CANNOT SAY from the information provided.

1. A financial year starts on March 31 and ends on April 1.

A   B   C

The statement is false because the passage states that a financial year starts on April 1 and ends on March 31. The statement is therefore **false.**

2. It can be said that the liquidity of both assets and liabilities is how easily they can be converted into cash.

A   B   C

The passage clearly states that both assets and liabilities are further classified based on their liquidity, that is, how easily they can be converted into cash. The correct answer is **true**.

3. A balance sheet is a legal requirement and every company must have one.

A   B   C

The passage makes no reference to this statement; therefore, **cannot say** is the correct answer.

HOW DID YOU SCORE?

26 – 30 = Excellent

21 – 25 = Above average

15 – 20 = Average

10 – 14 = Below average

0 – 9   = Well below average

If you did not perform too well during the test try not to worry. The important thing is to establish how you went wrong and to learn from the mistakes. This will enable you to gradually improve your scores.

Now move on to Verbal Reasoning Test 2. You have 10 minutes to complete the test which contains ten questions. Answers and explanations are provided at the end of the test.

TEST 2
VERBAL
REASONING

During Verbal Reasoning Test 2 there are 10 practice passages which each contain 3 questions. Answer each question based solely on the information provided. You must select either TRUE, FALSE or CANNOT SAY based on the information provided in the passage.

- You have 10 minutes to complete the test.

- Concentrate fully on each test.

- Circle the answer you believe to be correct.

- If unsure of an answer you should select the one that you believe to be correct.

- Avoid all forms of wild guessing.

Once you have completed the test check your answers with the ones that are provided.

1. Read the following text before answering the questions as either TRUE, FALSE or CANNOT SAY from the information given.

LEARNING THE TRAIN DRIVER'S ROUTE KNOWLEDGE

Competence in the train driver's route knowledge is extremely important, simply because trains have such a long stopping distance. As an example, a train travelling at a speed of 200 km/h can take three miles to stop. If the driver is unaware of his or her route knowledge, then stopping distances can be compromised. Stopping distances can be greatly affected by the weight of a train. Trains cannot be driven on line-of-sight like road vehicles because the driver has to know what is up-ahead in order to operate the train safely. This is why route knowledge is so important to the role of a train driver.

During initial training a trainee driver will be given a Route Learning Ticket. This gives the driver authority to travel in the cab whilst they learn the routes under supervision with a qualified instructor or qualified train driver. However, visual aids such as videos and visual learning platforms are being introduced so that the driver can learn the routes in a more controlled environment.

In order to successfully pass the route knowledge assessment a driver must learn all of the stations, speed restrictions, signals, signal boxes, level crossings, gradients and other features that are applicable to the role.

The assessment is either with a question and answer session in front of the manager or with a multiple choice route assessment package on a computer.

A – TRUE	B – FALSE	C – CANNOT SAY
Circle A if the question is TRUE from the information provided.	Circle B if the question is FALSE from the information provided.	Circle C if CANNOT SAY from the information provided.

1. A train's stopping distance is increased by the weight of the train.

   A   B   Ⓒ.

2. A train travelling at a speed of 400 km/h will take six miles to stop.

   A   B   Ⓒ.

3. Learning speed restrictions and stations will help towards passing the route knowledge assessment.

   A   B   Ⓒ

2. Read the following text before answering the questions as either TRUE, FALSE or CANNOT SAY from the information given.

SENDING FRANKED MAIL

You have the option of a one-off collection or a regular daily collection at a pre-arranged time. You can print and complete the form for a regular collection, or if you require a one-off collection or wish to discuss your collection requirements in more detail you can call the Business Relations Manager.

If you need to carry out an urgent same day mailing and would like your mail collected, you'll need to let us know before 12.00pm the same day by calling the Business Support telephone number. We will then arrange a single collection from your premises.

WEEKEND COLLECTIONS

We cannot collect on Saturdays or Sundays without prior arrangement. If you are interested in arranging a weekend collection for your business then please contact your allocated business support manager. A turnover in excess of £2500 per annum is required for this service.

PREPARING FRANKED MAIL FOR COLLECTION

1. Be sure to address your mail correctly, using the correct postcode and postage. Any franked mail inaccuracies will be rejected.

2. Bundle all franked mail together, with the addresses facing the same direction.

3. Bundle different types of mail separately.

4. Put stamped mail in separate bags.

5. Weigh each pouch, bag or tray, checking that they're less than 11kg (to comply with the health and safety limit).

6. Check that all your mail is ready for collection on time and at your collection point.

A – TRUE	**B – FALSE**	**C – CANNOT SAY**
Circle A if the question is TRUE from the information provided.	Circle B if the question is FALSE from the information provided.	Circle C if CANNOT SAY from the information provided.

1. Saturday collections can be arranged with prior arrangement.

   A   B   C

2. The health and safety limit for a bag of mail is 11kg.

   A   B   C

3. Bundled franked mail with the addresses that are not facing the same direction will be rejected.

   A   B   C

3. Read the following text before answering the questions as either TRUE, FALSE or CANNOT SAY from the information given.

BUSINESS FRANCHISE INFORMATION

Franchises are very popular at the moment with increasing numbers of people choosing to buy one as opposed to starting out by setting up their own business. By purchasing a franchise you are effectively taking advantage of the success of an already established business. As the 'franchisee', you are buying a licence to use the name, products, services, and management support systems of the "franchiser" company. This licence normally covers a particular geographical area and runs for a limited time. The downside to a franchise is that you will never actually legally own the business.

As a franchisee, the way you pay for the franchise may be through an initial fee, ongoing management fees, a share of your turnover, or a combination of these depending on how you have set up the franchise. A franchise business can take different legal forms - most are sole traders, partnerships or limited companies. Whatever the structure, the franchisee's freedom to manage the business is limited by the terms of the franchise agreement.

Is it worth investing in a business franchise? The simple answer is yes. However, it is important that you follow some careful steps before buying into a business franchise.

The good news is that there is information to suggest that the franchise business sector is still growing rapidly. During 2007 the NatWest Bank carried out a survey into the UK franchise market which revealed the astonishing financial growth of this sector. The approximate annual turnover of the business franchise sector is in excess of £10.8 billion.

What is more interesting to note is that the vast majority of business franchisees in 2007 were in profit - a total of 93% to be exact. In 1991 the total number of profitable franchisees was 70% and in 2004 it was 88%. Therefore, this business sector is growing and there is a reason for this.

A – TRUE	B – FALSE	C – CANNOT SAY
Circle A if the question is TRUE from the information provided.	Circle B if the question is FALSE from the information provided.	Circle C if CANNOT SAY from the information provided.

1. During 2007 the total number of business franchises that were not in profit totalled 7%.

 A   B   C

2. As the 'franchiser', you are buying a licence to use the name, products, services, and management support systems of the 'franchisee' company.

            A   B   C

3. A franchise business can take different legal forms including Limited Liability Partnership (LLP).

            A   B   C

4. Read the following text before answering the questions as either TRUE, FALSE or CANNOT SAY from the information given.

COMPANY ORDERING PROCESS

1.1 Our display of products and online services on our website is an invitation and not an offer to sell those goods to you.

1.2 An offer is made when you place the order for your products or online service. However, we will not have made a contract with you unless and until we accept your offer.

1.3 We take payment from your card when we process your order and have checked your card details. Goods are subject to availability. If we are unable to supply the goods, we will inform you of this as soon as possible. A full refund will be given if you have already paid for the goods. It is our aim to always keep our website updated and all goods displayed available.

1.4 If you enter a correct email address we will send you an order acknowledgement email immediately and receipt of payment. These do not constitute an order confirmation or order acceptance from us.

1.5 Unless we have notified you that we do not accept your order or you have cancelled it, order acceptance and the creation of the contract between you and us will take place at the point the goods you have ordered are dispatched from our premises to be delivered to the address you have given us.

1.6 The contract will be formed at the place of dispatch of the goods. All goods, wherever possible, will be dispatched within 24 hours of the order being placed, Monday to Thursday. If your order falls on a weekend or bank holiday, your order will be dispatched on the next available working day. All orders that are sent recorded delivery will require a signature. In the majority of cases, however, we will dispatch goods using Royal Mail's standard First Class delivery service.

A – TRUE	B – FALSE	C – CANNOT SAY
Circle A if the question is TRUE from the information provided.	Circle B if the question is FALSE from the information provided.	Circle C if CANNOT SAY from the information provided.

1. If a customer places an order, and they have entered a correct email address, they will immediately receive an order confirmation email.

   A   B   C

2. Orders placed on a Friday will be dispatched on a Saturday.

   A   B   C

3. Payment is taken from the card once the card details have been checked.

   A   B   C

5. Read the following text before answering the questions as either TRUE, FALSE or CANNOT SAY from the information given.

THE HISTORY OF FOOTBALL

The earliest records of a game similar to football as we know it today are from China in 206 BC and by AD 500 round footballs stuffed with hair were in use. It is suggested that Roman legions may have introduced the game to Europe and England in particular during the Roman occupation from AD 40 to AD 400.

The game increased in popularity, developing into 'mob games' called mêlées, or mellays, in which a ball, usually an inflated animal bladder, was advanced by kicking, punching and carrying. As many as 100 players from two towns or parishes started at a mid-point and used their localities' limits as goals. King Richard II of England banned the game in 1389 because it interfered with archery practice, and later monarchs issued similar proscriptions into the 15th Century, to little effect.

Football in a less violent form was played in England from the 17th Century by youths from wealthy and aristocratic families at public schools, although the authorities frowned on it as being too rowdy for young gentlemen. Rules varied from school to school, but all forbade running with the round ball or passing it forward.

By the middle of the 19th Century it was decided that uniformity of the rules was necessary so that every team could play the same game. Therefore the Football Association (FA) was formed in England and during the latter part of 1863, following a series of meetings, the first rules of the game of football were laid down. The first rules were based on those that had been in use at Cambridge University at the time. Some of the first rules also known as the Laws of the Game (there were 14 in total) included:

- Rule 1. The maximum length of the ground shall be 200 yards; the maximum breadth shall be 100 yards; the length and breadth shall be marked off with flags; and the goals shall be defined by two upright posts, 8 yards apart, without any tape or bar across them.

- Rule 10. Neither tripping nor hacking shall be allowed, and no player shall use his hands to hold or push an adversary.

- Rule 11. A player shall not throw the ball or pass it to another.

- Rule 14. No player shall be allowed to wear projecting nails, iron plates or gutta-percha on the soles or heels of his boots.

A – TRUE	**B – FALSE**	**C – CANNOT SAY**
Circle A if the question is TRUE from the information provided.	Circle B if the question is FALSE from the information provided.	Circle C if CANNOT SAY from the information provided.

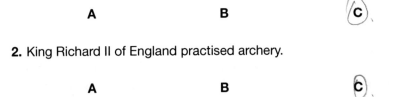

1. By the middle of the 19th Century it was decided that uniforms would be worn by referees.

   A   B   C

2. King Richard II of England practised archery.

   A   B   C

3. According to the passage there were four Laws of the Game.

   A   B   C

6. Read the following text before answering the questions as either TRUE, FALSE or CANNOT SAY from the information given.

RECONNAISSANCE

Reconnaissance is a crucial aspect of close protection activity, military operations, through to civilian protection from man-made and natural hazards used by meteorological and environmental services as well as a whole host of other agencies needing to ascertain risk of danger. These days the term is much more commonly replaced by `human intelligence' and practised by specialised units.

The word reconnaissance entered the English language around 1810 - not coincidentally of course during the period when the British were at war with Napoleon's French army. It derives from the French word literally meaning to `recognise'.

Reconnaissance refers to an operation whose objectives are to obtain information by employing a number of detection techniques. The information required for a close protection operative would centre around the identification, intent and risk component of a potential `enemy' securing evidence of their motivation methods and hence employing threat assessment and risk management strategies as part of the operational goals.

A close protection operative would, for example, use route reconnaissance, assessing a planned route of their principals' journey and identifying risk areas. A similar process would be employed in carrying out venue reconnaissance. Here a venue would be pre-checked by the close protection team, assessing the effectiveness of emergency exits and meeting points and implementing pre-planned strategies to deal with potential risk.

A – TRUE	B – FALSE	C – CANNOT SAY
Circle A if the question is TRUE from the information provided.	Circle B if the question is FALSE from the information provided.	Circle C if CANNOT SAY from the information provided.

1. A close protection team would pre-check a venue in order to assess the effectiveness of pre-planned strategies to deal with potential risk.

        A   B   C

2. Reconnaissance is often referred to as RECON within the industry.

        A   B   (C)

3. It is a coincidence that the word reconnaissance entered the English language during the period when the British were at war with France.

        A   B   C

7. Read the following text before answering the questions as either TRUE, FALSE or CANNOT SAY from the information given.

EQUALITY AND FAIRNESS IN THE FIRE SERVICE

Under the Race Relations (Amendment) Act, public authorities (including the Fire and Rescue Service) have a general duty to promote race equality. This means that when carrying out their functions or duties they must have due regard to the need to:

- Eliminate unlawful discrimination.

- Promote equality of opportunity.

- Promote good relations between persons of different racial groups.

In order to demonstrate how a Fire and Rescue Service plan to meet their statutory duties, they have an obligation to produce and publish what is called a Race Equality Scheme. The Race Equality Scheme outlines their strategy and action plan to ensure that equality and diversity are main-streamed through their policies, practices, procedures and functions. Central to this strategy are external consultation, monitoring and assessment, training, and ensuring that the public has access to this information.

"Equality is not about treating everybody the same, but recognising we are all individuals, unique in our own way. Equality and fairness is about recognising, accepting and valuing people's unique individuality according to their needs. This often means that individuals may be treated appropriately, yet fairly, based on their needs."

A – TRUE	B – FALSE	C – CANNOT SAY
Circle A if the question is TRUE from the information provided.	Circle B if the question is FALSE from the information provided.	Circle C if CANNOT SAY from the information provided.

1. Any form of racism is unwelcome in the Fire Service.

        A   **B**   **C**

2. The general public does have access to the Race Equality Scheme.

        A   **B**   **C**

3. The Fire Service may promote good relations between persons of different racial groups.

        A   **B**   **C**

8. Read the following text before answering the questions as either TRUE, FALSE or CANNOT SAY from the information given.

CENTRAL HEATING SYSTEM

Over half the money spent on fuel bills in the UK goes towards providing heating and hot water. Therefore, having an efficient boiler and central heating system is crucial to helping you to reduce costs. If your boiler and central heating system are in a poor state of repair, this can add up to an extra third on your heating bills.

In order to save money on your heating bills you must first of all understand your current system. The vast majority of homes in the UK have either a central heating system, consisting of a boiler and radiators, or they use electric storage heaters. This is the most common form of heating in the UK. A single boiler heats up water that is pumped through pipes to radiators throughout the house as well as providing hot water for the kitchen and bathroom taps.

Most boilers run on mains gas but, in areas where mains gas is not available, the boiler can run on oil, LPG (tank gas), coal or wood. Mains gas is usually the cheapest of these fuels, and it also has the lowest carbon dioxide emissions apart from wood.

Gas, oil and LPG boilers may be combination boilers, in which case they heat the hot water as it is needed and don't need to store it. Otherwise, the boiler heats up water and it is stored in a hot water cylinder that then feeds the taps. If you have a system like this, your options for energy-saving improvements include:

- replacing your current boiler with a more modern/efficient model.

- fitting better controls to your system.

- using the controls on your current system to only generate heat where and when you want it.

- switching to a cheaper or lower carbon fuel or technology such as wood-fuelled or solar water heating.

- making any insulation and draught-proofing improvements that you can.

A – TRUE	B – FALSE	C – CANNOT SAY
Circle A if the question is TRUE from the information provided.	Circle B if the question is FALSE from the information provided.	Circle C if CANNOT SAY from the information provided.

1. Most people in the UK are concerned about rising fuel bills.

      A   B   C

2. If your boiler and central heating system are in a poor state of repair, this can add over an extra third on your heating bills.

      A   B   C

3. If you have a combination boiler system your options for energy-saving improvements include fitting better controls to your system.

      A   B   C

9. Read the following text before answering the questions as either TRUE, FALSE or CANNOT SAY from the information given.

THE HISTORY OF THE SAS

The Special Air Service was originally founded by Lieutenant David Stirling during World War II. The initial purpose of the regiment was to be a long-range desert patrol group required to conduct raids and sabotage operations far behind enemy lines.

Lieutenant Stirling was a member of Number 8 Commando Regiment and he specifically looked for recruits who were both talented and individual specialists in their field, and who also had initiative.

The first mission of the SAS turned out to be a disaster. They were operating in support of Field Marshal Claude Auchinleck's attack in November 1941, but only 22 out of 62 SAS troopers deployed reached the rendezvous point. However, Stirling still managed to organise another attack against the German airfields at Aqedabia, Site and Agheila, which successfully destroyed 61 enemy aircraft without a single casualty. After that, the 1st SAS earned regimental status and Stirling's brother Bill began to arrange a second regiment called Number 2 SAS.

It was during the desert war that they performed a number of successful insertion missions and destroyed many aircraft and fuel depots in the process. Their success contributed towards Hitler issuing his Kommandobefehl order to execute all captured Commandos. The Germans then stepped up security and as a result the SAS changed their tactics. They used jeeps armed with Vickers K machine guns and used tracer ammunition to ignite fuel and aircraft. When the Italians captured David Stirling, he ended up in Colditz Castle as a prisoner of war for the remainder of the war. His brother, Bill Stirling, and 'Paddy' Blair Mayne, then took command of the regiment.

A – TRUE	B – FALSE	C – CANNOT SAY
Circle A if the question is TRUE from the information provided.	Circle B if the question is FALSE from the information provided.	Circle C if CANNOT SAY from the information provided.

1. During the SAS's first mission only 42 of the total troopers deployed reached the rendezvous point.

    A   B   C

2. When the Germans captured David Stirling, he ended up in Colditz Castle as a prisoner of war for the remainder of the war.

    A   B   C

3. Lieutenant Stirling was a member of Number 8 SAS Regiment.

    A   B   C

10. Read the following text before answering the questions as either TRUE, FALSE or CANNOT SAY from the information given.

HOW TO MEND A BICYCLE PUNCTURE

1. In order to mend a bicycle puncture you will first of all require a puncture repair kit, a pump, tyre levers, sandpaper, marking chalk and glue.

2. The first step is to stand the bike upside down on its saddle. Take off the effected wheel using the quick-release lever on the hub or, if the wheel is bolted on, undo with a spanner.

3. Take one of the tyre levers and slide the flat end between the rim and the tyre. Then, bend back the tyre lever and hook it on to one of the spokes. Take the next lever and do the same about 5 cm further around the tyre. Remove the first lever then move it further along the rim and use it to pry off the tyre again until one side is free.

4. Take the inner tube out and inflate. Check for thorns, wire or anything that may have caused the puncture. Take the tyre fully off the rim and inspect inside and outside for glass or debris. Check the rim to make sure no spoke ends have worn through the rim strip.

5. Hold the inflated tube to your ear: you may be able to hear air escaping. If you can't find the spot, hold part of the tube under water and watch for bubbles. Slowly move the tube through the water. Once you find the puncture, mark it with chalk or a crayon.

6. Dry the inner tube. Rough the area around the hole with sandpaper. Cover an area the size of a 20p coin around the puncture with glue. Leave until it gets tacky.

7. Place a patch centred over the puncture. Smooth out and make sure there are no air bubbles. Leave to dry for about 10 minutes.

8. Put one side of the tyre back on the rim. Place the tube back inside the tyre, beginning at the valve and working around the tyre. It should be slightly inflated.

9. Now, using the tyre levers, begin putting the free side of the tyre back inside the rim. Start near the valve and work the levers around in opposite directions. Be careful not to pinch the inner tube.

10. When you are left with about 15 cm still loose, it might be difficult to get the tyre back on. Use two tyre levers to keep each end of the loose bit of tyre in place, and then use the third to pop the tyre wall back inside the rim.

A – TRUE	**B – FALSE**	**C – CANNOT SAY**
Circle A if the question is TRUE from the information provided.	Circle B if the question is FALSE from the information provided.	Circle C if CANNOT SAY from the information provided.

1. A cause of punctures might be that spoke ends have worn through the rim strip.

   A   B   C

2. When putting the repaired wheel back onto the bicycle you will need to tighten the quick-release levers or redo the bolts with a spanner.

   A   B   C

3. When you place the tube back inside the tyre it should be slightly deflated.

   A   B   C

Now check your answers with the ones that follow. I have provided full explanations to the answers in order to assist you.

ANSWERS AND EXPLANATIONS TO VERBAL REASONING TEST 2

1. Read the following text before answering the questions as either TRUE, FALSE or CANNOT SAY from the information given.

LEARNING THE TRAIN DRIVER'S ROUTE KNOWLEDGE

Competence in the train driver's route knowledge is extremely important, simply because trains have such a long stopping distance. **2: As an example, a train travelling at a speed of 200 km/h can take three miles to stop.** If the driver is unaware of his or her route knowledge, then stopping distances can be compromised. **1: Stopping distances can be greatly affected by the weight of a train.** Trains cannot be driven on line-of-sight like road vehicles because the driver has to know what is up-ahead in order to operate the train safely. This is why route knowledge is so important to the role of a train driver.

During initial training a trainee driver will be given a Route Learning Ticket. This gives the driver authority to travel in the cab whilst they learn the routes under supervision with a qualified instructor or qualified train driver. However, visual aids such as videos and visual learning platforms are being introduced so that the driver can learn the routes in a more controlled environment.

3: In order to successfully pass the route knowledge assessment a driver must learn all of the stations, speed restrictions, signals, signal boxes, level crossings, gradients and other features that are applicable to the role.

The assessment is either with a question and answer session in front of the manager or with a multiple choice route assessment package on a computer.

A – TRUE	B – FALSE	C – CANNOT SAY
Circle A if the question is TRUE from the information provided.	Circle B if the question is FALSE from the information provided.	Circle C if CANNOT SAY from the information provided.

1. A train's stopping distance is increase by the weight of the train.

A   B   (C)

Whilst common sense would dictate that a train's stopping distance will increase by its weight we can only answer the question based on information provided. The passage states that stopping distances can be greatly affected by weight; however, it does not confirm that the stopping distance is increased by the effect of weight. Therefore, we must choose **cannot say**.

2. A train travelling at a speed of 400 km/h will take six miles to stop.

A   B   (C)

The passage states that a train travelling at a speed of 200km/h can take three miles to stop. You could be forgiven for assuming that a train travelling at 400 km/h would take six miles to stop. However, the passage does not confirm this and therefore we must select **cannot say** as the correct answer.

3. Learning speed restrictions and stations will help towards passing the route knowledge assessment.

                    B   C

The passage confirms that this statement is **true**.

2. Read the following text before answering the questions as either TRUE, FALSE or CANNOT SAY from the information given.

SENDING FRANKED MAIL

You have the option of a one-off collection or a regular daily collection at a pre-arranged time. You can print and complete the form for a regular collection, or if you require a one-off collection or wish to discuss your collection requirements in more detail you can call the Business Relations Manager.

If you need to carry out an urgent same day mailing and would like your mail collected, you'll need to let us know before 12.00pm the same day by calling the Business Support telephone number. We will then arrange a single collection from your premises.

WEEKEND COLLECTIONS

1: We cannot collect on Saturdays or Sundays without prior arrangement. If you are interested in arranging a weekend collection for your business then please contact your allocated business support manager. A turnover in excess of £2500 per annum is required for this service.

PREPARING FRANKED MAIL FOR COLLECTION

1. Be sure to address your mail correctly, using the correct postcode and postage. Any franked mail inaccuracies will be rejected.

2. **3: Bundle all franked mail together, with the addresses facing the same direction.**

3. Bundle different types of mail separately.

4. Put stamped mail in separate bags.

5. **2: Weigh each pouch, bag or tray, checking that they're less than 11kg (to comply with the health and safety limit).**

6. Check that all your mail is ready for collection on time and at your collection point.

A – TRUE	B – FALSE	C – CANNOT SAY
Circle A if the question is TRUE from the information provided.	Circle B if the question is FALSE from the information provided.	Circle C if CANNOT SAY from the information provided.

1. Saturday collections can be arranged with prior arrangement.

   B   C

The passage states that they cannot collect on Saturdays or Sundays without prior arrangement. Therefore, the statement is **true**.

2. The health and safety limit for a bag of mail is 11kg.

   B   C

The passage indicates that 11kg is the health and safety limit; therefore, the correct answer is **true**.

3. Bundled franked mail with the addresses that are not facing the same direction will be rejected.

   B   C

In part 1 of the *'preparing for franked mail collection'* section of the passage it states that any franked mail inaccuracies will be rejected. The statement is **true.**

3. Read the following text before answering the questions as either TRUE, FALSE or CANNOT SAY from the information given.

BUSINESS FRANCHISE INFORMATION

Franchises are very popular at the moment with increasing numbers of people choosing to buy one as opposed to starting out by setting up their own business. By purchasing a franchise you are effectively taking advantage of the success of an already established business. **2: As the 'franchisee', you are buying a licence to use the name, products, services, and management support systems of the 'franchiser' company.** This licence normally covers a particular geographical area and runs for a limited time. The downside to a franchise is that you will never actually legally own the business.

As a franchisee, the way you pay for the franchise may be through an initial fee, ongoing management fees, a share of your turnover, or a combination of these depending on how you have set up the franchise. **3: A franchise business can take different legal forms - most are sole traders, partnerships or limited companies.** Whatever the structure, the franchisee's freedom to manage the business is limited by the terms of the franchise agreement.

Is it worth investing in a business franchise? The simple answer is yes. However, it is important that you follow some careful steps before buying into a business franchise.

The good news is that there is information to suggest that the franchise business sector is still growing rapidly. During 2007 the NatWest Bank carried out a survey into the UK franchise market which revealed the astonishing financial growth of this sector. The approximate annual turnover of the business franchise sector is in excess of £10.8 billion. **1: What is more interesting to note is that the vast majority of business franchisees in 2007 were in profit - a total of 93% to be exact.** In 1991 the total number of profitable franchisees was 70% and in 2004 it was 88%. Therefore, this business sector is growing and there is a reason for this.

A – TRUE	**B – FALSE**	**C – CANNOT SAY**
Circle A if the question is TRUE from the information provided.	Circle B if the question is FALSE from the information provided.	Circle C if CANNOT SAY from the information provided.

1. During 2007 the total number of business franchises that were not in profit totalled 7%.

The passage states that 93% of business franchises in 2007 were in profit. This means that 7% were **not** in profit. The correct answer is **true**.

2. As the 'franchiser', you are buying a licence to use the name, products, services, and management support systems of the 'franchisee' company.

The passage states *"As the 'franchisee', you are buying a licence to use the name, products, services, and management support systems of the 'franchiser' company"*. The correct answer is **false**.

3. A franchise business can take different legal forms including Limited Liability Partnership (LLP).

A   B   (C)

We cannot state whether this sentence is true or false from the information provided. The passage states only that "a franchise business can take different legal forms". We cannot assume that this includes Limited Liability Partnerships (LLP). The correct answer is **cannot say**.

4. Read the following text before answering the questions as either TRUE, FALSE or CANNOT SAY from the information given.

COMPANY ORDERING PROCESS

1.1 Our display of products and online services on our website is an invitation and not an offer to sell those goods to you.

1.2 An offer is made when you place the order for your products or online service. However, we will not have made a contract with you unless and until we accept your offer.

1.3 3: **We take payment from your card when we process your order and have checked your card details.** Goods are subject to availability. If we are unable to supply the goods, we will inform you of this as soon as possible. A full refund will be given if you have already paid for the goods. It is our aim to always keep our website updated and all goods displayed available.

1.4 1: **If you enter a correct email address we will send you an order acknowledgement email immediately and receipt of payment. These do not constitute an order confirmation or order acceptance from us.**

1.5 Unless we have notified you that we do not accept your order or you have cancelled it, order acceptance and the creation of the contract between you and us will take place at the point the goods you have ordered are dispatched from our premises to be delivered to the address you have given us.

1.6 2: **The contract will be formed at the place of dispatch of the goods. All goods, wherever possible, will be dispatched within 24 hours of the order being placed, Monday to Thursday. If your order falls on a weekend or bank holiday, your order will be dispatched on the next available working day.** All orders that are sent recorded delivery will require a signature. In the majority of cases, however, we will dispatch goods using Royal Mail's standard First Class delivery service.

A – TRUE	B – FALSE	C – CANNOT SAY
Circle A if the question is TRUE from the information provided.	Circle B if the question is FALSE from the information provided.	Circle C if CANNOT SAY from the information provided.

1. If a customer places an order, and they have entered a correct email address, they will immediately receive an order confirmation email.

A   B   C

The passage states if a correct email address is entered they will send the customer an order acknowledgment email. It goes on to state that this email is not an order confirmation. The correct answer is **false**.

2. Orders placed on a Friday will be dispatched on a Saturday.

A   B   C

The passage states *"If your order falls on a weekend or bank holiday, your order will be dispatched on the next available working day"*. Although we could assume that the next 'working day' is Monday, this cannot be confirmed by the text in the passage. It could quite possibly be that the company classes Saturday as a working day. Therefore, the correct answer is **cannot say** based on the information provided.

3. Payment is taken from the card once the card details have been checked.

A   B   C

From the information provided in the passage we can confirm that this sentence is **true**.

5. Read the following text before answering the questions as either TRUE, FALSE or CANNOT SAY from the information given.

THE HISTORY OF FOOTBALL

The earliest records of a game similar to football as we know it today are from China in 206 BC and by AD 500 round footballs stuffed with hair were in use. It is suggested that Roman legions may have introduced the game to Europe and England in particular during the Roman occupation from AD 40 to AD 400.

The game increased in popularity, developing into 'mob games' called mêlées, or mellays, in which a ball, usually an inflated animal bladder, was advanced by kicking, punching and carrying. As many as 100 players from two towns or parishes started at a mid-point and used their localities' limits as goals. **2: King Richard II of England banned the game in 1389 because it interfered with archery practice,** and later monarchs issued similar proscriptions into the 15th Century, to little effect.

Football in a less violent form was played in England from the 17th Century by youths from wealthy and aristocratic families at public schools, although the authorities frowned on it as being too rowdy for young gentlemen. Rules varied from school to school, but all forbade running with the round ball or passing it forward.

1: By the middle of the 19th Century it was decided that uniformity of the rules was necessary so that every team could play the same game. Therefore the Football Association (FA) was formed in England and during the latter part of 1863, following a series of meetings, the first rules of the game of football were laid down. The first rules were based on those that had been in use at Cambridge University at the time. **3: Some of the first rules also known as the Laws of the Game (there were 14 in total) included:**

• Rule 1. The maximum length of the ground shall be 200 yards; the maximum breadth shall be 100 yards; the length and breadth shall be marked off with flags; and the goals shall be defined by two upright posts, 8 yards apart, without any tape or bar across them.

• Rule 10. Neither tripping nor hacking shall be allowed, and no player shall use his hands to hold or push an adversary.

• Rule 11. A player shall not throw the ball or pass it to another.

• Rule 14. No player shall be allowed to wear projecting nails, iron plates or gutta-percha on the soles or heels of his boots.

A – TRUE	**B – FALSE**	**C – CANNOT SAY**
Circle A if the question is TRUE from the information provided.	Circle B if the question is FALSE from the information provided.	Circle C if CANNOT SAY from the information provided.

1. By the middle of the 19th Century it was decided that uniforms would be worn by referees.

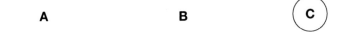

A   B   Ⓒ

Although the passage makes reference to the 19th Century and uniformity, it does not make reference to referees wearing uniforms. The correct answer is **cannot say** from the information provided.

2. King Richard II of England practised archery.

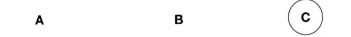

A   B   Ⓒ

This is a tricky one that may catch some people out! The passage states that King Richard II of England banned the game in 1389 because it interfered with archery practice. However, the passage does not state that it was he who practised archery. Therefore, the correct answer is **cannot say**.

3. According to the passage there were four Laws of the Game.

A   Ⓑ C

The sentence is **false**. The passage states that there were 14 Laws of the Game.

6. Read the following text before answering the questions as either TRUE, FALSE or CANNOT SAY from the information given.

RECONNAISSANCE

Reconnaissance is a crucial aspect of close protection activity, military operations, through to civilian protection from man-made and natural hazards used by meteorological and environmental services as well as a whole host of other agencies needing to ascertain risk of danger. These days the term is much more commonly replaced by `human intelligence' and practised by specialised units.

3: The word reconnaissance entered the English language around 1810 - not coincidentally of course during the period when the British were at war with Napoleon's French army. It derives from the French word literally meaning to `recognise'.

Reconnaissance refers to an operation whose objectives are to obtain information by employing a number of detection techniques. The information required for a close protection operative would centre around the identification, intent and risk component of a potential `enemy' securing evidence of their motivation methods and hence employing threat assessment and risk management strategies as part of the operational goals.

A close protection operative would, for example, use route reconnaissance, assessing a planned route of their principals' journey and identifying risk areas. A similar process would be employed in carrying out venue reconnaissance. **1: Here a venue would be pre-checked by the close protection team, assessing the effectiveness of emergency exits and meeting points and implementing pre-planned strategies to deal with potential risk.**

A –TRUE	B – FALSE	C – CANNOT SAY
Circle A if the question is TRUE from the information provided.	Circle B if the question is FALSE from the information provided.	Circle C if CANNOT SAY from the information provided.

1. A close protection team would pre-check a venue in order to assess the effectiveness of pre-planned strategies to deal with potential risk.

       B   **C**

From the information provided in the passage we can confirm that this statement is **true**.

2. Reconnaissance is often referred to as RECON within the industry.

A   **B**   **C**

Although the phrase RECON is commonly used within the industry we are unable to confirm this as fact from the passage. The correct answer is **cannot say.**

3. It is a coincidence that the word reconnaissance entered the English language during the period when the British were at war with France.

A   

The passage states that it is not a coincidence the word entered the English language during the period when the British were at war with Napoleon's French army. Therefore, the correct answer is **false**.

7. Read the following text before answering the questions as either TRUE, FALSE or CANNOT SAY from the information given.

EQUALITY AND FAIRNESS IN THE FIRE SERVICE

Under the Race Relations (Amendment) Act, public authorities (including the Fire and Rescue Service) have a general duty to promote race equality. 3: This means that when carrying out their functions or duties they must have due regard to the need to:

- Eliminate unlawful discrimination.

- Promote equality of opportunity.

- Promote good relations between persons of different racial groups.

In order to demonstrate how a Fire and Rescue Service plan to meet their statutory duties, they have an obligation to produce and publish what is called a Race Equality Scheme. The Race Equality Scheme outlines their strategy and action plan to ensure that equality and diversity are mainstreamed through their policies, practices, procedures and functions. 2: Central to this strategy are external consultation, monitoring and assessment, training, and ensuring that the public has access to this information.

"Equality is not about treating everybody the same, but recognising we are all individuals, unique in our own way. Equality and fairness is about recognising, accepting and valuing people's unique individuality according to their needs. This often means that individuals may be treated appropriately, yet fairly, based on their needs."

A – TRUE	B – FALSE	C – CANNOT SAY
Circle A if the question is TRUE from the information provided.	Circle B if the question is FALSE from the information provided.	Circle C if CANNOT SAY from the information provided.

1. Any form of racism is unwelcome in the Fire Service.

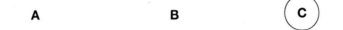

This statement is certainly true; however, the passage makes no reference to this and, as such, **cannot say** is the correct answer.

2. The general public does have access to the Race Equality Scheme.

The passage states that central to the strategy is ensuring that the public has access to this information. The statement is **true.**

3. The Fire Service may promote good relations between persons of different racial groups.

A   (B) C

The statement states that the Fire Service may promote good relations between persons of different racial groups, whereas the passage states they must promote good relations. The correct answer is **false.**

8. Read the following text before answering the questions as either TRUE, FALSE or CANNOT SAY from the information given.

CENTRAL HEATING SYSTEM

Over half the money spent on fuel bills in the UK goes towards providing heating and hot water. Therefore, having an efficient boiler and central heating system is crucial to helping you to reduce costs. **2: If your boiler and central heating system are in a poor state of repair, this can add up to an extra third on your heating bills.**

In order to save money on your heating bills you must first of all understand your current system. The vast majority of homes in the UK have either a central heating system, consisting of a boiler and radiators, or they use electric storage heaters. This is the most common form of heating in the UK. A single boiler heats up water that is pumped through pipes to radiators throughout the house as well as providing hot water for the kitchen and bathroom taps.

Most boilers run on mains gas but, in areas where mains gas is not available, the boiler can run on oil, LPG (tank gas), coal or wood. Mains gas is usually the cheapest of these fuels, and it also has the lowest carbon dioxide emissions apart from wood.

3: Gas, oil and LPG boilers may be combination boilers, in which case they heat the hot water as it is needed and don't need to store it. Otherwise, the boiler heats up water and it is stored in a hot water cylinder that then feeds the taps. If you have a system like this, your options for energy-saving improvements include:

- replacing your current boiler with a more modern/efficient model.

- fitting better controls to your system.

- using the controls on your current system to only generate heat where and when you want it.

- switching to a cheaper or lower carbon fuel or technology such as wood-fuelled or solar water heating.

- making any insulation and draught-proofing improvements that you can.

A –TRUE	B – FALSE	C – CANNOT SAY
Circle A if the question is TRUE from the information provided.	Circle B if the question is FALSE from the information provided.	Circle C if CANNOT SAY from the information provided.

1. Most people in the UK are concerned about rising fuel bills.

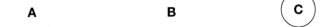

A   B   C

The passage does make reference to heating bills but not in respect of the statement. The answer is **cannot say** based on the information provided.

2. If your boiler and central heating system are in a poor state of repair, this can add over an extra third on your heating bills.

A   B C

The passage states *"If your boiler and central heating system are in a poor state of repair, this can add up to an extra third on your heating bills."* Because the statement refers to it adding over an extra third on your heating bills the correct answer is **false**.

3. If you have a combination boiler system your options for energy-saving improvements include fitting better controls to your system.

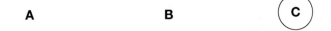

A   B   C

In respect of energy saving improvements and fitting netter controls to your system, the passage is referring to systems where the water is stored in a hot water cylinder. We cannot tell from the information in the passage if the same applies to combination boiler systems. Therefore, the correct answer is **cannot say.**

9. Read the following text before answering the questions as either TRUE, FALSE or CANNOT SAY from the information given.

THE HISTORY OF THE SAS

The Special Air Service was originally founded by Lieutenant David Stirling during World War II. The initial purpose of the regiment was to be a long-range desert patrol group required to conduct raids and sabotage operations far behind enemy lines.

3: Lieutenant Stirling was a member of Number 8 Commando Regiment and he specifically looked for recruits who were both talented and individual specialists in their field, and who also had initiative.

1: The first mission of the SAS turned out to be a disaster. They were operating in support of Field Marshal Claude Auchinleck's attack in November 1941, but only 22 out of 62 SAS troopers deployed reached the rendezvous point. However, Stirling still managed to organise another attack against the German airfields at Aqedabia, Site and Agheila, which successfully destroyed 61 enemy aircraft without a single casualty. After that, the 1st SAS earned regimental status and Stirling's brother Bill began to arrange a second regiment called Number 2 SAS.

It was during the desert war that they performed a number of successful insertion missions and destroyed many aircraft and fuel depots in the process. Their success contributed towards Hitler issuing his Kommandobefehl order to execute all captured Commandos. The Germans then stepped up security and as a result the SAS changed their tactics. They used jeeps armed with Vickers K machine guns and used tracer ammunition to ignite fuel and aircraft. 2: When the Italians captured David Stirling, he ended up in Colditz Castle as a prisoner of war for the remainder of the war. His brother, Bill Stirling, and 'Paddy' Blair Mayne, then took command of the regiment.

A – TRUE	B – FALSE	C – CANNOT SAY
Circle A if the question is TRUE from the information provided.	Circle B if the question is FALSE from the information provided.	Circle C if CANNOT SAY from the information provided.

1. During the SAS's first mission only 42 of the total troopers deployed reached the rendezvous point.

A   B C

According to the passage only 22 out of 62 troopers deployed reached the rendezvous point. The answer is **false.**

2. When the Germans captured David Stirling, he ended up in Colditz Castle as a prisoner of war for the remainder of the war.

A   B C

The passage states that the Italians captured David Stirling, not the Germans. The correct answer is **false.**

3. Lieutenant Stirling was a member of Number 8 SAS Regiment.

A   B C

Lieutenant Stirling was a member of Number 8 Commando Regiment, not Number 8 SAS Regiment. The correct answer is **false.**

10. Read the following text before answering the questions as either TRUE, FALSE or CANNOT SAY from the information given.

HOW TO MEND A BICYCLE PUNCTURE

1. In order to mend a bicycle puncture you will first of all require a puncture repair kit, a pump, tyre levers, sandpaper, marking chalk and glue.

2. The first step is to stand the bike upside down on its saddle. **2: Take off the effected wheel using the quick-release lever on the hub or, if the wheel is bolted on, undo with a spanner.**

3. Take one of the tyre levers and slide the flat end between the rim and the tyre. Then, bend back the tyre lever and hook it on to one of the spokes. Take the next lever and do the same about 5 cm further around the tyre. Remove the first lever then move it further along the rim and use it to pry off the tyre again until one side is free.

4. Take the inner tube out and inflate. Check for thorns, wire or anything that may have caused the puncture. Take the tyre fully off the rim and inspect inside and outside for glass or debris. **1: Check the rim to make sure no spoke ends have worn through the rim strip.**

5. Hold the inflated tube to your ear: you may be able to hear air escaping. If you can't find the spot, hold part of the tube under water and watch for bubbles. Slowly move the tube through the water. Once you find the puncture, mark it with chalk or a crayon.

6. Dry the inner tube. Rough the area around the hole with sandpaper. Cover an area the size of a 20p coin around the puncture with glue. Leave until it gets tacky.

7. Place a patch centred over the puncture. Smooth out and make sure there are no air bubbles. Leave to dry for about 10 minutes.

8. **3: Put one side of the tyre back on the rim. Place the tube back inside the tyre, beginning at the valve and working around the tyre. It should be slightly inflated.**

9. Now, using the tyre levers, begin putting the free side of the tyre back inside the rim. Start near the valve and work the levers around in opposite directions. Be careful not to pinch the inner tube.

10. When you are left with about 15 cm still loose, it might be difficult to get the tyre back on. Use two tyre levers to keep each end of the loose bit of tyre in place, and then use the third to pop the tyre wall back inside the rim.

A – TRUE	B – FALSE	C – CANNOT SAY
Circle A if the question is TRUE from the information provided.	Circle B if the question is FALSE from the information provided.	Circle C if CANNOT SAY from the information provided.

1. A cause of punctures might be that spoke ends have worn through the rim strip.

   B   **C**

The passage states that you should "Check the rim to make sure no spoke ends have worn through the rim strip". The correct answer is **true**.

2. When putting the repaired wheel back onto the bicycle you will need to tighten the quick-release levers or redo the bolts with a spanner.

A   **B**

The passage only makes reference to taking off the wheel, not replacing it. Therefore, the correct answer is **cannot say** based on the information provided in the passage.

3. When you place the tube back inside the tyre it should be slightly deflated.

A

The passage states that it should be slightly inflated not deflated. The correct answer is **false.**

HOW DID YOU SCORE?

26 – 30 = Excellent

21 – 25 = Above average

15 – 20 = Average

10 – 14 = Below average

0 – 9   = Well below average

So far, you have been used to answering just three sub questions. During the next verbal reasoning test there are five tests that each contains five sub-questions. You will need to work faster in order to complete the test. You have 10 minutes to complete this test. Answers and explanations are provided at the end of the test.

TEST 3
VERBAL
REASONING

During Verbal Reasoning Test 3 there are 10 practice passages which each contain 5 questions. Answer each question based solely on the information provided. You must select either TRUE, FALSE or CANNOT SAY based on the information provided in the passage.

- You have 10 minutes to complete the test.
- Concentrate fully on each test.
- Circle the answer you believe to be correct.
- If unsure of an answer you should select the one that you believe to be correct.
- Avoid all forms of wild guessing.

Once you have completed the test check your answers with the ones that are provided.

1. Read the following text before answering the questions as either TRUE, FALSE or CANNOT SAY from the information given.

DETAILS OF THE MEDICAL

Applicants who successfully complete the online assessment, the physical aptitude test and the interview will be invited to attend a medical assessment. Applicants must satisfy all medical requirements in order to progress to the next stage. Details of the medical are as follows:

HEALTH QUESTIONNAIRE • applicants will be required to accurately answer questions regarding their medical history.

PHYSICAL EXAMINATION • applicants will be required to successfully pass a medical examination by the Medical Officer which includes, amongst others, the following five elements:

- Lung function test.

- Hearing test.

- Vision test (including colour vision).

- Urine test.

- Pathology test.

TIME • the entire employment medical assessment will take approximately 1½ hours to complete.

SUPPORTING MEDICAL INFORMATION • applicants with pre-existing medical conditions are encouraged to bring medical reports, x-rays or other medical information to assist the Medical Officer in assessing their individual case.

CONFIDENTIALITY • all medical information collected as part of the medical assessment will be considered confidential, and will be released only with the specific written consent of the applicant, or in accordance with legal requirements.

Once the applicant has successfully passed the medical they will be invited to the next stage of the selection process.

A – TRUE	B – FALSE	C – CANNOT SAY
Circle A if the question is TRUE from the information provided.	Circle B if the question is FALSE from the information provided.	Circle C if CANNOT SAY from the information provided.

1. There are 5 different elements to the medical.

　　　　　　A　　　　　　　　B　　　　　　　　C

2. The physical examination will take 1½ hours to complete.

　　　　　　A　　　　　　　　B　　　　　　　　C

3. Applicants with pre-existing medical conditions must take with them x-rays and medical reports to assist the Medical Officer.

　　　　　　A　　　　　　　　B　　　　　　　　C

4. The next stage of the selection process, upon successful completion of the medical, is the interview.

　　　　　　A　　　　　　　　B　　　　　　　　C

5. The release of confidential information collected by the Medical Officer during the medical is illegal.

　　　　　　A　　　　　　　　B　　　　　　　　C

2. Read the following text before answering the questions as either TRUE, FALSE or CANNOT SAY from the information given.

AUSTRALIAN BUSHFIRES

The summers in Australia can bring total devastation to many through the many bushfires which occur. Bushfires destroy livelihoods, property, machinery, eucalyptus forests and they can even spread to the suburban areas of major cities.

Although all bushfires can have a devastating effect, few of them fall under the 'disaster' category. Some of these were in:

- **Victoria (2009): 173 lives were lost in this bushfire, so it is more commonly referred to as Black Saturday.**

- **South Australia and Victoria (1983): This claimed 76 lives and was named Ash Wednesday.**

- **Southern Victoria (1969): 23 lives were claimed.**

- **New South Wales (1968): There were 14 fatalities in this bushfire in the Blue Mountains and coastal region.**

- Hobart and Southern Tasmania (1967): 62 people were killed.

- **Victoria (1939): This was named Black Friday after 71 people lost their lives.**

There are two different types of bushfires in Australia - grass fires and forest fires. Grass fires more commonly occur on grazing and farm land. These often destroy fences, livestock, machinery and they sometimes claim lives. Forest fires are largely made up of eucalyptus trees. These are extremely difficult to control due to the high amounts of flammable vapour from the leaves. The bushfires are fought by large numbers of trained volunteer fire-fighters. Helicopters and light aircraft are sometimes used to make observations about the fire and some also have the capacity to carry water. Aircraft used to carry water in order to extinguish forest fires often find that the visibility is extremely poor, preventing them from getting close enough to the fire in order to extinguish it with their quantities of water.

Aircraft used to make observations about the fire are used to:

- establish which direction the fire is travelling
- locating suitable grid references to make fire-breaks to prevent firespread
- locating nearby homes, businesses, other buildings and livestock that are in danger from the fire spreading.

A – TRUE	B – FALSE	C – CANNOT SAY
Circle A if the question is TRUE from the information provided.	Circle B if the question is FALSE from the information provided.	Circle C if CANNOT SAY from the information provided.

1. Bushfires are extinguished by large numbers of full-time trained fire-fighters.

A   B   C

2. In total there have been 419 fatalities from Australian bushfires since 1939.

A   B   C

3. Hundreds of animals are killed by the bushfires each year.

A   B   C

4. Aircraft deployed to extinguish bushfires struggle to get close to the fire due to the poor visibility.

A   B   C

5. One way to prevent a bushfire from spreading is to create a fire-break.

A   B   C

3. Read the following text before answering the questions as either TRUE, FALSE or CANNOT SAY from the information given.

AVIEMORE RAIL INCIDENT

The time is 6:37pm on Sunday the 7th of February 2010. A two-car diesel multiple unit, which has been travelling on the West Highland Line in Scotland heading towards Aviemore, has derailed and caught fire as a result. One carriage has been left in a precarious position on the 40-foot high embankment whilst the remaining three carriages have come to rest blocking both the upside and downside tracks. In addition to blocking the lines, the incident has also caused the closure of the A35 road which is located directly below the rail line.

The train involved in the incident is a First ScotRail Class 120 Turbostar unit 156TGE. The driver of the train is a 52-year-old male named as George McDermott and the train's headcode is 6Y56. Witnesses claim that the train derailed after hitting a large boulder which had come to rest on the track following a landslide. In total, there are 34 passengers on the four carriage train. There are a number of injuries to casualties. Amongst others, an elderly female who is 72-year-old is suffering from a suspected broken collar-bone; a 32-year-old male is suffering from a serious head injury and a 21-year-old pregnant female is suffering from shock and a broken finger. The Rail Control Centre has informed all oncoming trains of the incident and has operated red stop signals along the route.

The weather is severely hampering rescue operations and the Fire and Rescue Commander has indicated that there could be a significant delay before all casualties are safely removed from the scene. The local weather centre has forecast gales of up to 60 miles per hour over the next 12 hours with temperatures dropping to minus 3 degrees.

A – TRUE	B – FALSE	C – CANNOT SAY
Circle A if the question is TRUE from the information provided.	Circle B if the question is FALSE from the information provided.	Circle C if CANNOT SAY from the information provided.

1. The current temperature is minus 3 degrees.

A   B   C

2. The train involved in the incident is a First ScotRail Class 120 Turbostar unit 6Y56.

A   B   C

3. A train derailment is when the train inadvertently leaves the track.

A   B   C

4. In total there are three passengers injured.

A   B   C

5. The A35 has been affected by the incident.

A   B   C

4. Read the following text before answering the questions as either TRUE, FALSE or CANNOT SAY from the information given.

THE DEFINITION AND PURPOSE OF THE JOB

A Trainee Probation Officer is an employee of the Probation Area, appointed on a time-limited (normally two-year) contract, who is working to obtain the Diploma in Probation Studies (DipPS). Upon successful completion of training and the award of the DipPS, a Trainee Probation Officer will be eligible for appointment as a Probation Officer.

THE MAIN DUTIES AND RESPONSIBILITIES

As a person in training, the Trainee Probation Officer's principal objective is to undertake the academic work and gain the experience in probation practice necessary to acquire, practise and demonstrate the knowledge, skills, values and competencies required to obtain both the degree and the NVQ, which together constitute the DipPS. The Trainee Probation Officer's learning needs will determine the amount and nature of the work undertaken.

In the course of their training, Trainee Probation Officers will undertake work on behalf of the employing Probation Area and will, therefore, provide a service to courts, penal institutions, individual Probation Area users (or persons for whom the Probation Area has a responsibility) and local communities. A Trainee Probation Officer will, therefore, be required at all times to work in accordance with the Probation Rules, National Standards, the Probation Board's policies and all other relevant enactments and policies. In particular, in all their work, Trainee Probation Officers will ensure that service delivery reflects the Probation Area's Equality of Opportunities and Anti-Discriminatory policies and will promote, especially by contributing to risk assessment and management, the Area's overriding responsibility to ensure the safety of service users, staff and the public.

Specifically, a Trainee Probation Officer will:

- Attend all required academic teaching events, as arranged by the University, the Consortium or the Probation Area.

- Complete the required academic assignments.

- Observe and participate in training and other learning experiences as arranged by the Consortium or the Probation Area.

- Undertake such work on the Probation Area's behalf as may be required.

A – TRUE	B – FALSE	C – CANNOT SAY
Circle A if the question is TRUE from the information provided.	Circle B if the question is FALSE from the information provided.	Circle C if CANNOT SAY from the information provided.

1. NVQ stands for 'National Vocational Qualification'.

      A   B   C

2. Trainee Probation Officers will carry out work on behalf of the employing Probation Area during their training.

      A   B   C

3. During training a Trainee Probation Officer may miss some academic teaching events.

      A   B   C

4. The main goal of the Trainee Probation Officer is to carry out he necessary work and gain sufficient experience in order to obtain the degree and NVQ that forms part of the DipPS.

      A   B   C

5. Trainee Probation Officers must ensure that the service they deliver is representative of the Probation Area's equality policy.

      A   B   C

5. Read the following text before answering the questions as either TRUE, FALSE or CANNOT SAY from the information given.

ACCOUNT BILLING INFORMATION

There are two separate options offered for account billing:

Monthly* - This option operates on a 4-week cycle beginning on the day of account activation

Annual - This option operates on a 365-day cycle beginning on the day of account activation

Note: *Customers on a monthly billing cycle are billed every 4 weeks.

When your account reaches its appropriate billing day (your account's expiration date) your credit card will be automatically billed for the next billing cycle and your account expiration date will be extended by an additional 4 weeks (or 365 for annual packages) and you will receive a receipt via email. If the transaction is unsuccessful for any reason, we will attempt to re-bill your credit card for 2 consecutive days and send an unsuccessful renewal email for each unsuccessful attempt (to your accounts specified Billing Profile email address).

After your first unsuccessful renewal attempt your account status will be updated to Billing Hold Level 1. This status indicates that your account is overdue but otherwise has no direct effect on your service which will continue for up to 4 weeks following your actual expiration date.

4 Weeks Past Account Expiration
4 weeks after your account expires we will attempt to re-bill your credit card for two monthly payments. If successful your account expiration date will be extended by an additional 4 weeks (from bill date) and you will receive a receipt via email.

If unsuccessful your account status will be updated to Billing Hold Level 2. This status indicates that your account is now more than 4 weeks overdue and will close all account service until payment has been received. We will attempt to re-bill your credit card for 2 consecutive days and send an unsuccessful renewal email for each unsuccessful attempt.

When your account is in this status you will still be able to log in and access both the Earn Cash page (to manage affiliate referrals) and the Renew Account page.

56 Days Past Account Expiration

56 days after your account expires we will attempt to re-bill your credit card for three monthly payments. If successful your account expiration date will be extended by an additional 4 weeks (from bill date), your account will be reactivated and you will receive a receipt via email. If unsuccessful your account will be permanently closed.

A – TRUE	B – FALSE	C – CANNOT SAY
Circle A if the question is TRUE from the information provided.	Circle B if the question is FALSE from the information provided.	Circle C if CANNOT SAY from the information provided.

1. The accounts expiration date can be determined as the billing day.

A   B   C

2. Billing Hold Level 2 occurs when an attempt to take two monthly payments after an account is 4 weeks past account expiration fails.

A   B   C

3. Customers who opt for the monthly billing option will be billed every 4 weeks on the first day of each month.

A   B   C

4. For the annual billing option the first expiration date will be 365 days after account activation.

A   B   C

5. Billing Hold Level 1 occurs after the first successful renewal attempt.

A   B   C

Now that you have completed the test check your answers with the ones that follow in the next section.

ANSWERS AND EXPLANATIONS TO VERBAL REASONING TEST 3

1. Read the following text before answering the questions as either TRUE, FALSE or CANNOT SAY from the information given.

DETAILS OF THE MEDICAL

4: Applicants who successfully complete the online assessment, the physical aptitude test and the interview will be invited to attend a medical assessment. Applicants must satisfy all medical requirements in order to progress to the next stage. Details of the medical are as follows:

HEALTH QUESTIONNAIRE • applicants will be required to accurately answer questions regarding their medical history.

PHYSICAL EXAMINATION • applicants will be required to successfully pass a medical examination by the Medical Officer **1: which includes, amongst others, the following five elements:**

• Lung function test.

• Hearing test.

• Vision test (including colour vision).

• Urine test.

• Pathology test.

TIME • **2: the entire employment medical assessment will take approximately 1½ hours to complete.**

SUPPORTING MEDICAL INFORMATION • **3: applicants with pre-existing medical conditions are encouraged to bring medical reports, x-rays or other medical information to assist the Medical Officer in assessing their individual case.**

CONFIDENTIALITY • **5: all medical information collected as part of the medical assessment will be considered confidential, and will be released only with the specific written consent of the applicant, or in accordance with legal requirements.**

Once the applicant has successfully passed the medical they will be invited to the next stage of the selection process.

A – TRUE	B – FALSE	C – CANNOT SAY
Circle A if the question is TRUE from the information provided.	Circle B if the question is FALSE from the information provided.	Circle C if CANNOT SAY from the information provided.

1. There are 5 different elements to the medical.

The passage states that, **amongst others**, the following five elements are examined. Therefore, there are *more* than five different elements to the medical and so the answer is **false**.

2. The physical examination will take 1½ hours to complete.

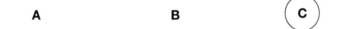

The passage states it will approximately 1½ hours to complete the entire medical assessment. We cannot determine from this information how long the physical examination part of the assessment will take; therefore, the answer is **cannot say** from the information provided.

3. Applicants with pre-existing medical conditions must take with them x-rays and medical reports to assist the Medical Officer.

The passage states that applicants are 'encouraged' to bring these with them, not that they 'must'. The answer is **false**.

4. The next stage of the selection process, upon successful completion of the medical, is the interview.

The passage confirms that the interview is conducted prior to the medical. Therefore, the correct answer is **false**.

5. The release of confidential information collected by the Medical Officer during the medical is illegal.

      A   **B**   **C**

Although the passage does make reference to 'legal requirements', it does not state what exactly the legal requirements are. The correct answer is **cannot say** based on the information provided.

2. Read the following text before answering the questions as either TRUE, FALSE or CANNOT SAY from the information given.

AUSTRALIAN BUSHFIRES

The summers in Australia can bring total devastation to many through the many bushfires which occur. 3: Bushfires destroy livelihoods, property, machinery, eucalyptus forests and they can even spread to the suburban areas of major cities.

Although all bushfires can have a devastating effect, few of them fall under the 'disaster' category. 2: Some of these were in:

• Victoria (2009): 173 lives were lost in this bushfire, so it is more commonly referred to as Black Saturday.

• South Australia and Victoria (1983): This claimed 76 lives and was named Ash Wednesday.

• Southern Victoria (1969): 23 lives were claimed.

• New South Wales (1968): There were 14 fatalities in this bushfire in the Blue Mountains and coastal region.

• Hobart and Southern Tasmania (1967): 62 people were killed.

• Victoria (1939): This was named Black Friday after 71 people lost their lives.

There are two different types of bushfires in Australia - grass fires and forest fires. Grass fires more commonly occur on grazing and farm land. These often destroy fences, livestock, machinery and they sometimes claim lives. Forest fires are largely made up of eucalyptus trees. These are extremely difficult to control due to the high amounts of flammable vapour from the leaves. 1: The bushfires are fought by large numbers of trained volunteer fire-fighters. Helicopters and light aircraft are sometimes used to make observations about the fire and some also have the capacity to carry water. 4: Aircraft used to carry water in order to extinguish forest fires often find that the visibility is extremely poor, preventing them from getting close enough to the fire in order to extinguish it with their quantities of water.

Aircraft used to make observations about the fire are used to:

- establish which direction the fire is travelling

- **5: locating suitable grid references to make fire-breaks to prevent firespread**

- locating nearby homes, businesses, other buildings and livestock that are in danger from the fire spreading.

A – TRUE	B – FALSE	C – CANNOT SAY
Circle A if the question is TRUE from the information provided.	Circle B if the question is FALSE from the information provided.	Circle C if CANNOT SAY from the information provided.

1. Bushfires are extinguished by large numbers of full-time trained fire-fighters.

A   B   C

The passage states that the bushfires are fought by a large number of trained volunteer fire-fighters, there is no discussion about the number of hours they do. Therefore, the statement is **false**.

2. In total there have been 419 fatalities from Australian bushfires since 1939.

A   B   C

The total number of fatalities listed in the passage does equal 419. However, the passage also states that 'some of these were in' the disaster category. Therefore, we cannot confirm whether or not 419 is the total figure as there are clearly other disasters. The correct answer is **cannot say** based on the information provided.

3. Hundreds of animals are killed by the bushfires each year.

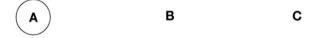

The passage makes no reference to this claim. The passage only mentions that animals are destroyed by bushfires each year but makes no reference to numbers involved. The correct answer is **cannot say** based on the information provided.

4. Aircraft deployed to extinguish bushfires struggle to get close to the fire due to the poor visibility.

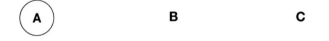

The passage states that aircraft used to carry water in order to extinguish forest fires often find that the visibility is poor, preventing them from getting close to the fire. The correct answer is **true**.

5. One way to prevent a bushfire from spreading is to create a fire-break.

This statement is **true**. The passage makes reference to aircraft being used to make observations in order to locate suitable grid references in order to make fire-breaks which will prevent fire spreading.

3. Read the following text before answering the questions as either TRUE, FALSE or CANNOT SAY from the information given.

AVIEMORE RAIL INCIDENT

The time is 6:37pm on Sunday the 7th of February 2010. A two-car diesel multiple unit, which has been travelling on the West Highland Line in Scotland heading towards Aviemore, has derailed and caught fire as a result. One carriage has been left in a precarious position on the 40-foot high embankment whilst the remaining three carriages have come to rest blocking both the upside and downside tracks. **5: In addition to blocking the lines, the incident has also caused the closure of the A35 road which is located directly below the rail line.**

2: The train involved in the incident is a First ScotRail Class 120 Turbostar unit 156TGE. The driver of the train is a 52-year-old male named as George McDermott and the train's headcode is 6Y56. Witnesses claim that the train derailed after hitting a large boulder which had come to rest on the track following a landslide. In total, there are 34 passengers on the four carriage train. **4: There are a number of injuries to casualties. Amongst others, an elderly female who is 72-year-old is suffering from a suspected broken collar-bone; a 32-year-old male is suffering from a serious head injury and a 21-year-old pregnant female is suffering from shock and a broken finger.** The Rail Control Centre has informed all oncoming trains of the incident and has operated red stop signals along the route.

The weather is severely hampering rescue operations and the Fire and Rescue Commander has indicated that there could be a significant delay before all casualties are safely removed from the scene. **1: The local weather centre has forecast gales of up to 60 miles per hour over the next 12 hours with temperatures dropping to minus 3 degrees.**

A –TRUE	B – FALSE	C – CANNOT SAY
Circle A if the question is TRUE from the information provided.	Circle B if the question is FALSE from the information provided.	Circle C if CANNOT SAY from the information provided.

1. The current temperature is minus 3 degrees.

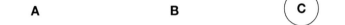

A   B   C

The passage states that "the local weather centre has forecast gales of up to 60 miles per hour over the next 12 hours with temperatures dropping to minus 3 degrees". Although the passage makes reference to the temperature dropping to minus 3 degrees, this does not confirm the current temperature. Based on the lack of information in the passage the correct answer is **cannot say**.

2. The train involved in the incident is a First ScotRail Class 120 Turbostar unit 6Y56.

A   B C

This statement is **false.** The passage states that "The train involved in the incident is a First ScotRail Class 120 Turbostar unit 156TGE". The difference between the two is the unit numbers supplied at the end.

3. A train derailment is when the train inadvertently leaves the track.

A   B   C

Although this statement is factually correct, the passage makes no reference to what a derailment actually is. Therefore, the correct answer is **cannot say** based on the information provided.

4. In total there are three passengers injured.

A   B C

The passage does provide details of injuries to three passengers. However, it also states "amongst others". Therefore, the correct answer is **false** as there are more than three injuries in total according to the passage.

5. The A35 has been affected by the incident.

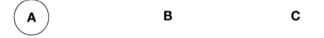

        (A)   B   C

The passage indicates that the incident has caused the closure of the A35 road. The statement is therefore **true.**

4. Read the following text before answering the questions as either TRUE, FALSE or CANNOT SAY from the information given.

THE DEFINITION AND PURPOSE OF THE JOB

A Trainee Probation Officer is an employee of the Probation Area, appointed on a time-limited (normally two-year) contract, who is working to obtain the Diploma in Probation Studies (DipPS). Upon successful completion of training and the award of the DipPS, a Trainee Probation Officer will be eligible for appointment as a Probation Officer.

THE MAIN DUTIES AND RESPONSIBILITIES

4: As a person in training, the Trainee Probation Officer's principal objective is to undertake the academic work and gain the experience in probation practice necessary to acquire, practise and demonstrate the knowledge, skills, values and competencies required to obtain both the degree and the NVQ, which together constitute the DipPS. The Trainee Probation Officer's learning needs will determine the amount and nature of the work undertaken.

1: In the course of their training, Trainee Probation Officers will undertake work on behalf of the employing Probation Area and will, therefore, provide a service to courts, penal institutions, individual Probation Area users (or persons for whom the Probation Area has a responsibility) and local communities. A Trainee Probation Officer will, therefore, be required at all times to work in accordance with the Probation Rules, National Standards, the Probation Board's policies and all other relevant enactments and policies. 5: In particular, in all their work, Trainee Probation Officers will ensure that service delivery reflects the Probation Area's Equality of Opportunities and Anti-Discriminatory policies and will promote, especially by contributing to risk assessment and management, the Area's overriding responsibility to ensure the safety of service users, staff and the public.

Specifically, a Trainee Probation Officer will:

- 3: Attend all required academic teaching events, as arranged by the University, the Consortium or the Probation Area.

- Complete the required academic assignments.

- Observe and participate in training and other learning experiences as arranged by the Consortium or the Probation Area.

- 2: Undertake such work on the Probation Area's behalf as may be required.

A – TRUE	**B – FALSE**	**C – CANNOT SAY**
Circle A if the question is TRUE from the information provided.	Circle B if the question is FALSE from the information provided.	Circle C if CANNOT SAY from the information provided.

1. NVQ stands for 'National Vocational Qualification'.

A B 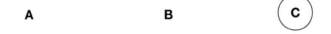 C

Yes, NVQ does stand for National Vocational Qualification. However, the passage makes no reference to this fact. Therefore, the correct answer must be **cannot say** based on the information provided.

2. Trainee Probation Officers will carry out work on behalf of the employing Probation Area during their training.

 A B C

The passage clearly indicates that in the course of their training, Trainee Probation Officers will undertake work on behalf of the employing Probation Area. The statement is therefore **true**.

3. During training a Trainee Probation Officer may miss some academic teaching events.

A  B C

The passage states that a Trainee Probation Officers will attend all academic teaching events. The statement is **false** based on the information provided in the passage.

4. The main goal of the Trainee Probation Officer is to carry out he necessary work and gain sufficient experience in order to obtain the degree and NVQ that forms part of the DipPS.

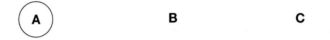

The passage confirms that the principal objective of a Trainee Probation Officer is to undertake the academic work and gain the experience in probation practice necessary to acquire, practise and demonstrate the knowledge, skills, values and competencies required to obtain both the degree and the NVQ, which together constitute the DipPS. Therefore, the statement is **true**.

5. Trainee Probation Officers must ensure that the service they deliver is representative of the Probation Area's equality policy.

The passage clearly states that Trainee Probation Officers will ensure that service delivery reflects the Probation Area's Equality of Opportunities and Anti-Discriminatory policies. The correct answer is **true**.

5. Read the following text before answering the questions as either TRUE, FALSE or CANNOT SAY from the information given.

ACCOUNT BILLING INFORMATION

There are two separate options offered for account billing:

Monthly* - This option operates on a 4-week cycle beginning on the day of account activation.

Annual - This option operates on a 365-day cycle beginning on the day of account activation.

Note: *Customers on a monthly billing cycle are billed every 4 weeks.

1: When your account reaches its appropriate billing day (your account's expiration date) your credit card will be automatically billed for the next billing cycle and **4: your account expiration date will be extended by an additional 4 weeks (or 365 for annual packages)** and you will receive a receipt via email. If the transaction is unsuccessful for any reason, we will attempt to re-bill your credit card for 2 consecutive days and send an unsuccessful renewal email for each unsuccessful attempt (to your accounts specified Billing Profile email address).

After your first unsuccessful renewal attempt your account status will be updated to Billing Hold Level 1. This status indicates that your account is overdue but otherwise has no direct effect on your service which will continue for up to 4 weeks following your actual expiration date.

4 Weeks Past Account Expiration
2: 4 weeks after your account expires we will attempt to re-bill your credit card for two monthly payments. If successful your account expiration date will be extended by an additional 4 weeks (from bill date) and you will receive a receipt via email. If unsuccessful your account status will be updated to Billing Hold Level 2. This status indicates that your account is now more than 4 weeks overdue and will close all account service until payment has been received. We will attempt to re-bill your credit card for 2 consecutive days and send an unsuccessful renewal email for each unsuccessful attempt.

When your account is in this status you will still be able to log in and access both the Earn Cash page (to manage affiliate referrals) and the Renew Account page.

56 Days Past Account Expiration

56 days after your account expires we will attempt to re-bill your credit card for three monthly payments. If successful your account expiration date will be extended by an additional 4 weeks (from bill date), your account will be reactivated and you will receive a receipt via email. If unsuccessful your account will be permanently closed.

A – TRUE	B – FALSE	C – CANNOT SAY
Circle A if the question is TRUE from the information provided.	Circle B if the question is FALSE from the information provided.	Circle C if CANNOT SAY from the information provided.

1. The accounts expiration date can be determined as the billing day.

   B   C

The passage confirms that the billing day is also known as the account's expiration date. Therefore, the statement is **true.**

2. Billing Hold Level 2 occurs when an attempt to take two monthly payments after an account is 4 weeks past account expiration fails.

The passage makes it clear that 4 weeks after the account expires they will attempt to re-bill the credit card for two monthly payments. It also goes on to state that if the transaction is unsuccessful the status will be updated to Billing Hold Level 2. The statement is therefore **true** based on this information.

3. Customers who opt for the monthly billing option will be billed every 4 weeks on the first day of each month.

This is a difficult one! The passage states that the monthly billing option *"operates on a 4-week cycle beginning on the day of account activation"*.

You could be forgiven for selecting false as your answer. However, because we do not know for sure which day each customer has activated their account, we cannot confirm that any of them will be billed on any other day than the first of each month. Whilst it is highly unlikely that all customers will have signed up on the first day of each month, we cannot say for certain this is the case. Therefore, based on the information provided we must select **cannot say** as the correct answer.

4. For the annual billing option the first expiration date will be 365 days after account activation.

     A   **B**   **C**

The passage states that the expiration date for annual billing option is 365 days. The correct answer is **true.**

5. Billing Hold Level 1 occurs after the first successful renewal attempt.

         A    **B** **C**

The correct answer is **false**. Billing Hold Level 1 occurs after the first unsuccessful renewal attempt, not successful.

HOW DID YOU SCORE?

44 – 50 = Excellent

35 – 43 = Above average

25 – 34 = Average

16 – 24 = Below average

0 – 15   = Well below average

Congratulations on reaching this far in the guide! Now move on to the final mock exam and let's see how much you have improved since the start.

FINAL MOCK EXAM
VERBAL REASONING

During the final mock exam there are 12 practice passages which each contain 5 questions. Answer each question based solely on the information provided. You must select either TRUE, FALSE or CANNOT SAY based on the information provided in the passage.

- You have 12 minutes to complete the entire mock exam.

- Concentrate fully on each test.

- Circle the answer you believe to be correct.

- If unsure of an answer you should select the one that you believe to be correct.

- Avoid all forms of wild guessing.

Once you have completed the exam check your answers with the ones that are provided at the end.

1. Read the following text before answering the questions as either TRUE, FALSE or CANNOT SAY from the information given.

FACTS ABOUT ANTARCTICA

Very few people ever travel to Antarctica, which is one of the seven continents on the Earth. The reason is because Antarctica is so cold and icy that it is a very inhospitable place for human life. It is a very fascinating place, with lots of amazing wildlife in the surrounding waters.

Some of the many interesting facts about Antarctica include:

- Antarctica, along with the Arctic, is one of the two coldest places on Earth. It is located very close to the South Pole, while the Arctic is to the north.

- One third of all the fresh water on the entire planet is located on Antarctica.

- There are absolutely no trees on this icy continent.

- The temperature rarely gets above freezing, so that the entire area is covered in ice and snow. In fact, the ice and snow is one mile deep in most spots and in some areas it is up to three miles deep.

- Very few creatures live on the actual land; in fact the largest creature that resides directly on Antarctica is the midge. Midges are only half an inch long. There are many living creatures in the water surrounding the land, however.

- The lowest temperature ever recorded on Antarctica was in 1983. It was -129 degrees Fahrenheit.

- Codfish in the waters surrounding Antarctica actually have antifreeze flowing through their blood because the water is so cold.

- No single country has claimed ownership over Antarctica. In fact, all of the countries have agreed to joint ownership and everyone is able to send scientific research missions to the area.

- No native people reside on the land, as it would be near impossible for humans to live there for an extended period of time.

- Many people think of Antarctica as a place where it snows continuously, when it fact it rarely snows each year. Instead, the appearance of snowstorms is caused by existing snow that blows off of the ground by hard winds.

- For a large part of the history of the Earth, Antarctica was a warm continent.

While people do not reside on this ice cold land, some people do go there for research projects and other exploratory missions. It is a vast and beautiful land and much of its beauty is because it is untouched by industrialisation and the damage that humans can inflict.

A – TRUE	B – FALSE	C – CANNOT SAY
Circle A if the question is TRUE from the information provided.	Circle B if the question is FALSE from the information provided.	Circle C if CANNOT SAY from the information provided.

1. Antarctica is owned by a single country.

A B C

2. The temperature on Antarctica sometimes rises above freezing.

A B C

3. It is impossible for humans to live on Antarctica for long periods of time.

A B C

4. Antarctica is yet to be affected by industrialisation.

A B C

5. The Arctic is one of the coldest places on Earth.

A B C

2. Read the following text before answering the questions as either TRUE, FALSE or CANNOT SAY from the information given.

THE QUALITIES OF A GOOD TEACHER

There is no question that teaching is one of the most important careers in the UK. Our teachers are helping to shape the future of our population, as they are training our children to enter the workforce and become the leaders of tomorrow. Without teachers there would be no formal education for our youth in the UK. Many people want to be a teacher, but a large number find that it is just not for them. Not just anyone can be a good teacher, because it takes certain qualities and personality traits to teach children of all ages.

Those who are the best teachers often have certain aspects to their personalities that enable them to command the attention and respect of their students. Some of the qualities that make up a good teacher include:

- Patience - Patience is by far the most vital aspect of a teacher's personality. In order to keep calm and cool when children are misbehaving, a teacher must have extreme patience. This is especially important when handling younger children, as they can often be difficult to control.

- Intelligence - Of course, in order for a teacher to properly instruct their students, they must be well-versed in the subject that they are teaching. They must be able to give their students the right information and to be prepared to answer any questions that their pupils may come up with.

- Creativity - In order to make lessons more interesting and to engage the students, a teacher must use creativity. Good teachers are able to think of clever ways to present the materials that need to be learned so that children actually want to learn.

- Organisation - Teachers must be organised, as they have a lot of things that they must juggle. They have to keep track of the lessons that they have taught and what they have coming up, they have to keep a hold on papers that they need to grade and they also must have all of the necessary hand-outs for each of their classes.

- Leadership –Teachers are required to lead their pupils. They must be able to stand in front of the classroom with confidence, so that the children trust and respect them and are willing to be led.

Being a teacher is one of the hardest careers in the world and being good at it is even more challenging. A good teacher will be able to demonstrate all of the above qualities on a daily basis.

A – TRUE	B – FALSE	C – CANNOT SAY
Circle A if the question is TRUE from the information provided.	Circle B if the question is FALSE from the information provided.	Circle C if CANNOT SAY from the information provided.

1. In total there are five different qualities that make up a good teacher.

A   B   C

2. Patience is not the most important attribute of a teacher's personality.

A   B   C

3. Most people find that teaching is not for them.

A   B   C

4. Teaching is not a particularly well paid job.

A   B   C

5. Younger children are often the easiest to control.

A   B   C

3. Read the following text before answering the questions as either TRUE, FALSE or CANNOT SAY from the information given.

THE EVOLUTION OF MAN

Evolution is a widely studied science that many scientific leaders have researched and pondered over for many years. For the most part, these scientists believe that human beings evolved from Order Primates. This group includes chimpanzees, monkeys, gorillas and lemurs. They have gathered their information by studying fossils that have been unearthed from all over the world, with the oldest dating back more than 5 million years ago. Humans evolved because of diet and environmental factors, among other things. Many stages of man have been identified and here we will explain each of them.

The earliest stage of man included such species as Australopithecus anamensis, Australopithecus robustus, Australopithecus africanus and Australopithecus boisei. Australopithecus anamensis is identified as a species that walked on two feet. Australopithecus africanus had a larger brain than other species at the time and seemed to have developed molars and canine teeth, as did the Australopithecus robustus, indicating that both ate things that required more chewing and grinding than before.

Then came along Homo habilis. This species had a much larger brain size than the Australopithecus, which enabled the species to invent tools that they could use for making things and killing prey. Homo habilis may have been able to speak and was about 5 feet tall and weighed around 100 lbs.

The next species to come along was Homo erectus, who had an even larger brain size than Hobo habilis. Erectus was also taller (about 5 feet 5 inches) and this is attributed to the fact that he was smarter and able to hunt for meat. The meat made Erectus grow larger and stronger.

Homo sapiens (Archaic) were next in the evolution of man. Fossils have been found all over the world and scientists can determine from these that he had an even larger brain, which enabled him to reason, speak, make plans and control how he moved his body. He is believed to have been a socialised being that used various weapons and tools.

THE **TESTING** SERIES

Homo sapiens neanderthalensis were the next evolution of man, leading to our species today. This species appeared at the very end of the ice age and they were able to survive in very cold weather, because of their body size, which retained more body heat. They had even more social skills than the species before them, as well as a very strong and muscular build. The evolution of man was a long process, over approximately 5 million years, which resulted in the humans that reside on Earth today.

A – TRUE	B – FALSE	C – CANNOT SAY
Circle A if the question is TRUE from the information provided.	Circle B if the question is FALSE from the information provided.	Circle C if CANNOT SAY from the information provided.

1. Homo erectus evolved prior to Homo habilis.

A   B   C

2. Homo sapiens were capable of controlling their own body movement.

A   B   C

3. The human race is more than 5 million years old.

A   B   C

4. Homo habilis was able to speak.

A   B   C

5. Homo erectus was capable of eating meat.

A   B   C

4. Read the following text before answering the questions as either TRUE, FALSE or CANNOT SAY from the information given.

THE DIFFERENCE BETWEEN AFFECT AND EFFECT

Not everyone is skilled with grammar and even those who are struggle with some of the most commonly mistaken words in the English language. Two words that cause a lot of confusion for people are affect and effect. Many people have a lot of trouble with the usage and the meanings of these words, as they are very easy to mix up. The majority of people aren't really sure of when to use one or the other, which is why they simply end up guessing.

The reason why these two words are so confusing is that while each is a different part of speech, they sometimes function as other parts of speech. In most cases, affect is a verb and effect is a noun. You can affect something, which will produce an effect on that thing. Things are always affected, never effected. This is the general rule that you should always remember. Only in rare cases will affect or effect serve as different parts of speech. Remember that an effect is always something that is produced and an affect is what you do to something.

Just to be thoroughly confusing, there are very rare situations when effect will be used as a verb and affect will be used as a noun. For the most part, you will never have to use them in these cases. Use the general rule from above (affect is a verb and effect is a noun), but try to remember the following odd instances. As a verb, effect means to accomplish, produce or execute something. As a noun, affect is used by psychologists to refer to desires and emotions as factors in how someone acts or thinks. Obviously, both of these instances do not occur often, but you will see them sometimes in things you may be reading, such as an academic journal. Always keep in your mind that under most circumstances, use affect as a verb and effect as a noun.

A – TRUE	B – FALSE	C – CANNOT SAY
Circle A if the question is TRUE from the information provided.	Circle B if the question is FALSE from the information provided.	Circle C if CANNOT SAY from the information provided.

1. In most cases, effect is a verb and affect is a noun.

           A   B   C

2. If something is affected there will be a resultant effect on it.

           A   B   C

3. There are occasions when effect will be used as a verb and affect will be used as a noun.

           A   B   C

4. Affect can be described as what you do to something.

           A   B   C

5. Affect is always something that is produced and an effect is what you do to something.

           A   B   C

5. Read the following text before answering the questions as either TRUE, FALSE or CANNOT SAY from the information given.

MOUNT EVEREST

Mount Everest is one of the most famous natural landmarks in the world; it is the highest point above sea level on Earth. Many mountain climbers seek to climb Mount Everest as their ultimate goal and people visit in droves every single year to test their climbing skills on this peak. Here are some facts about Mount Everest to help you understand more about the mountain and its history.

- Everest is about 29,000 feet above sea level.

- The mountain was actually named by British surveyors for George Everest. He was a famous Surveyor General of India throughout the mid-nineteenth century.

- Everest has been altered considerably by five major glaciers, which still continue to change how the mountain looks. Glaciers have been credited with turning the mountain into a massive pyramid with three large ridges and three faces. The best time to climb Everest is at the beginning of May. This will ensure that the monsoon season is avoided.

- In 1975, the largest expedition to climb Everest was completed. A group of 410 people from China scaled the mountain together.

- One of the biggest problems that people face when climbing Everest is the extreme climate. The temperatures on the mountain never get above freezing and in the dead of winter they are well within negative temperatures. Climbers have to prepare not only for the lack of oxygen at altitude, but also for the incredibly cold temperatures.

- Everest is rising 1/3 of an inch every single year. It is also very slowly moving northeastward, at about 3 inches per year.

- Climbers Peter Habeler and Reinhold Messner have the distinction of being the first people to climb the mountain without supplemental oxygen. They did this in 1978.

- The safest year for climbers on Mount Everest was 1993. This is because 129 climbers made it all the way to the summit, with 8 deaths.

- 1996 is considered the least safe year on the mountain. 98 climbers made it to the summit, yet 15 died.

- The mountain is considered very sacred by those in Tibet and Nepal. In Tibet, Mount Everest is called Chomolangma, which means *'Goddess Mother of Snows',* in the Tibetan language. Those in Nepal refer to the mountain as Sagarmatha, which means *'Mother of the Universe'.*

A – TRUE	B – FALSE	C – CANNOT SAY
Circle A if the question is TRUE from the information provided.	Circle B if the question is FALSE from the information provided.	Circle C if CANNOT SAY from the information provided.

1. The monsoon season starts after the month of May.

A   B   C

2. Everest is increasing in height each year.

A   B   C

3. To some people in Nepal, Mount Everest is also called Chomolangma, which means *'Goddess Mother of Snows'.*

A   B   C

4. Everest is the tallest mountain in the world.

A   B   C

5. George Everest worked in India during the mid-nineteenth century.

A   B   C

6. Read the following text before answering the questions as either TRUE, FALSE or CANNOT SAY from the information given.

THE CAMINO DE SANTIAGO

The Camino de Santiago was a major Christian pilgrimage route to the Cathedral of Santiago de Compostela in northwestern Spain. It dates back to medieval times and is still in existence today. This historic pilgrimage route has many interesting and unique things about it. Here are some facts and figures related to the Camino de Santiago:

- In English, The Camino de Santiago means The Way of Saint James, which is how many in the English-speaking world refer to this historic route.

- The Camino has been a Christian route for more than 1,000 years and many believe that it was used for other purposes long before that.

- The Camino was named as the very first European Cultural Route in 1987 by the Council of Europe. It is also one of UNESCO's World Heritage Sites.

- The symbol of the Camino de Santiago is the scallop shell. There are differing stories as to why, but many believe it is because the shell has multiple grooves that come together at a single point. This is a metaphor for how people came down many paths to end up at the Camino de Santiago.

- The earliest records of visitors to the Cathedral date back all the way to the 8th century.

- Pilgrims who travelled the route purchased a "credencial", or pilgrim's passport, from the Spanish government so that they could safely travel the route. They could show their passport at various pilgrim's hostels along the way in Spain and France, where they could stay overnight.

- Pilgrims who completed the walk along the Camino de Santiago were given a certificate of accomplishment called the Compostela. They had to walk at least 100 km in order to achieve this, but it was a very big honour for the devout people that had travelled to the Cathedral.

- Every day at noon, a pilgrim's mass is held at the Cathedral of Santiago de Compostela in honour of the pilgrims.

- On special Holy Years, more pilgrims than ever take the route. The last Holy Year was 2010, when more than 272,000 pilgrims walked the route to the Cathedral. The next Holy Year is in 2021. Holy Years are when the sacred holiday of Saint James's Day (July 25), falls on a Sunday.

The Camino de Santiago is a very famous and historical route that people today still travel to get to the Cathedral of Santiago de Compostela.

A – TRUE	B – FALSE	C – CANNOT SAY
Circle A if the question is TRUE from the information provided.	Circle B if the question is FALSE from the information provided.	Circle C if CANNOT SAY from the information provided.

1. Pilgrims are the people who walk the Camino de Santiago.

A B C

2. The next Holy Year will be 2012.

A B C

3. The Camino de Santiago is 100 km long.

A B C

4. A credencial is a pilgrim's passport that enables them to travel safely.

A B C

5. People have been walking the Camino de Santiago since the 8th century.

A B C

7. Read the following text before answering the questions as either TRUE, FALSE or CANNOT SAY from the information given.

THE EUROPEAN UNION

The European Union was officially established in 1993 under its current name. The history of the EU and its current actions are something that many people are not fully aware of. Here are some interesting facts and figures about the European Union.

- The Maastricht Treaty of 1993 formally named the European Union.

- The EU traces its roots all the way back to European Coal and Steel Community and the European Economic Community, formed together by six member countries in 1958.

- The EU has a combined population of 500 million inhabitants in 27 member states. This is 7.3% of the world's population.

- The eurozone, which is a monetary union within the European Union, was established in 1999. There are 17 member states in the eurozone, all of which utilise the euro as their form of currency. This enables free spending in all of the eurozone countries without having to exchange currencies, making movement from country to country much easier.

- There are many important institutions of the EU, such as the European Commission, Council of the European Union, the European Council, the European Central Bank, and the Court Justice of the European Union.

- European Parliament is part of the legislative function of the EU and members are directly elected from each member country every 5 years.

- The anthem of the European Union is *"Ode to Joy"*.

- In the entire organisation there are 23 different languages spoken.

- The euro currency was introduced on January 1, 2002, where it was printed and distributed throughout 12 member countries. This was a huge logistical operation, with nearly 80 billion coins involved.

- 38,000 people are employed by the European Commission.

- 1% of the annual budget of the EU is spent on staff and administration, as well as continued maintenance on buildings.

- The European Commission is hailed as having one of the largest translation centres in the world, with 1,750 linguists. There are also 600 support staff members for the linguists.

- European Parliament holds its regular committee meetings in Brussels.

- The EU has the world's third largest population, after China and India.

- The EU's GDP is now bigger than that of the US.

The European Union has certainly grown immensely since it was officially named in 1993. 12 member states were added since 2004 and the population and economic impact continues to grow.

A – TRUE	B – FALSE	C – CANNOT SAY
Circle A if the question is TRUE from the information provided.	Circle B if the question is FALSE from the information provided.	Circle C if CANNOT SAY from the information provided.

1. There are currently 12 countries using the euro currency.

      A   B   C

2. There are more people living in the European Union than China.

      A   B   C

3. 7.3% of the world's population live in the European Union.

      A   B   C

4. Greece is in the European Union.

      A   B   C

5. One of the benefits of the eurozone is that it negates the need to change currency between the different countries that form part of it.

      A   B   C

8. Read the following text before answering the questions as either TRUE, FALSE or CANNOT SAY from the information given.

RULES OF AMERICAN FOOTBALL

American football is an incredibly popular sport all over the United States, but it is less popular throughout other countries. An increasing number of people in the UK are starting to play and watch this classic American sport. If you want to be able to play, or understand the sport while watching it on television, you need to know the rules. Here is an overview of the basic rules of American football.

Offense and Defense

Each team has 11 players on the field at one time. The team that has possession of the football is the offense, and their objective is to advance the ball down the field. They do this by running with the ball, or passing it to another team-mate. They score points when they get to the very end of the field, crossing the goal line into the end zone. The team that does not have the ball is the defense. Their objective is to prevent the other team from getting into the end zone and scoring a touchdown. They do this by attempting to block players from catching passes, tackling players who are running with the ball, and/or trying to catch passes that are intended for the offensive team (catching such a pass is called an interception).

If the offensive team scores, or if they lose possession of the ball to the defense, then the two teams switch roles. This continues on until the four timed quarters of the game have been completed. The game is divided into four 15-minute quarters, along with a half-time break of 12 minutes. The teams change ends of the field after each quarter.

The Field

A football field measures 100 yards long and is 53 yard wide. There are markers on the field to tell the players, coaches and officials which yard line they are on. Every 10 yards is marked by a line. The end zone is also marked and is at the 0-yard line on the field. This zone is 10 yards long, but does not count towards the 100 yards of the field.

Moving the Ball Down the Field

The offensive team must do their best to gain as much 'yardage' before they are stopped by a tackle or an out of bounds movement. With each ten yards the offense progresses, they get what is called a first down.

If they pass the ball and it is incomplete or someone fumbles and they do not gain any yards, this is a second down. The team has four tries (or downs) to get the ball down the field before they must give up possession. If they are on their second, third or fourth down and make it 10 yards, they start over at a first down.

Scoring
If the offense makes it to the end zone, they score a touchdown, which is six points. They can then either kick a field goal for an extra point, or they can do a small play in the last 10 yards of the field which is called a two-point conversion and is worth two points. If they do not score a touchdown and decide to try for a field goal, they can score three points. There are many other intricate rules of American football, but the above are all of the most important aspects.

A – TRUE	**B – FALSE**	**C – CANNOT SAY**
Circle A if the question is TRUE from the information provided.	Circle B if the question is FALSE from the information provided.	Circle C if CANNOT SAY from the information provided.

1. In American Football you can only score points via a touchdown when the ball crosses the goal line into the end zone.

    A   B   C

2. When a team does not have the ball they are the defense.

    A   B   C

3. The game of American Football, excluding breaks, is 60 minutes in duration.

    A   B   C

4. The protective helmets worn by American Footballers are designed to protect the head from injury.

          A   **B**   **C**

5. A football field measures 100 yards wide and 53 yards long.

          A   **B**   **C**

9. Read the following text before answering the questions as either TRUE, FALSE or CANNOT SAY from the information given.

FACTS ABOUT THE NATIONAL GEOGRAPHIC

The National Geographic Society (NGS) is a group that is headquartered in Washington, DC in the United States, which publishes a magazine titled National Geographic. The group and the fascinating magazine it releases are very interesting to many people all over the world, as they have made huge strides in environmental and historical preservation, among other things.

- The National Geographic Society was founded on January 27, 1888 by Gardiner Greene Hubbard.

- Worldwide membership of the society is currently at about 8.5 million people.

- The current president since 1998 is John M. Fahey, Jr.

- The logo for the NGS is a rectangular yellow portrait frame, which can be found as its television logo and on the margins surrounding the front cover of their magazine.

- The organisation is designed to fund research and preservation of historical, archaeological, and natural science areas throughout the entire world. It is a non-profit organisation.

- The Society has given grants for scientific research since it began, and recently gave out its 10,000th grant.

- The NGS began as a group for elite world travellers and academics that were wealthy and interested in advancing tourism and interest in history, science and culture.

- In 2004, the NGS headquarters in Washington, DC was one of the first buildings ever to receive a Green Certification from Global Green USA.

- The magazine started nine months after the society was founded in October 1888. It is published 12 times per year, along with at least four supplements.

- More than 50 million readers all over the world read National Geographic every month, in 32 different languages.

- NGS has funded more than 9,600 conservation, research and exploration projects throughout the entire Earth.

- In addition to the magazine, NGS reaches more than 400 million people per month through videos, their television channel, books, radio, music, films, interactive media and more.

- National Geographic won the 'Magazine of the Year' award from the American Society of Magazine Editors in 2011, the top award any magazine can receive.

- The magazine has tackled such issues as environmentalism, endangered species, global warming, chemical pollution, deforestation and so much more.

- National Geographic has held an annual photography competition since 2006, with people competing in 18 different countries.

A –TRUE	B – FALSE	C – CANNOT SAY
Circle A if the question is TRUE from the information provided.	Circle B if the question is FALSE from the information provided.	Circle C if CANNOT SAY from the information provided.

1. More than 50 million readers all over the world read National Geographic every year, in 32 different languages.

A   B   C

2. The National Geographic Society's magazine is not titled National Geographic.

A   B   C

3. The National Geographic Society has 50 million members all over the world in 32 different languages.

A   B   C

4. The National Geographic Society was founded over 100 years ago.

A   B   C

5. The National Geographic Society is a profitable business.

A   B   C

10. Read the following text before answering the questions as either TRUE, FALSE or CANNOT SAY from the information given.

INTERNAL COMBUSTION ENGINE THEORY

Internal combustion engines are the most commonly used engines in the entire world. They are used in a wide range of vehicles and chances are if you drive a car, yours uses this type of engine. They are also used in industrial applications and largely replaced the steam engine throughout the 20th century.

What is the theory?

The main principle behind any type of internal combustion engine is if you put a small amount of a type of high-energy fuel, such as gasoline, into a very small space and ignite it, a large amount of energy will be released in the form of gas that expands. This energy can then be used to propel almost anything and it is very effective. This is why the majority of common vehicle engines are built based upon this theory. This principle is the core that most car engines today are built on.

How it works

The engine utilises a fossil fuel inside of a combustion chamber and combines this with an oxidiser, which is usually air. When the air and the fossil fuel are heated in the combustion chamber, the gas and the air will expand. The expansion of the gas and the air when combustion is applied causes a force to the pistons, turbine blades, or nozzle inside of the engine. This then transforms the chemical energy of the internal combustion energy into mechanical energy that powers the vehicle or industrial application.

Most cars on the roads right now use a four-stroke combustion cycle. This converts gasoline so that it can propel the car forward. This is also called the 'Otto Cycle', as it is named after the inventor, Nikolaus Otto, who invented it in 1867. These four strokes are called the intake stroke, compression stroke, combustion stroke, and the exhaust stroke.

The first internal combustion engine was created by Jean Joseph Étienne Lenoir, a Belgian engineer, in 1859. Without his application of the theory, we might not have the advanced vehicle engines we have today.

A – TRUE	B – FALSE	C – CANNOT SAY
Circle A if the question is TRUE from the information provided.	Circle B if the question is FALSE from the information provided.	Circle C if CANNOT SAY from the information provided.

1. The majority of vehicle engines are built based upon the internal combustion engine theory.

    A   B   C

2. The first internal combustion engine was built in Belgium.

    A   B   C

3. Without the internal combustion engine we would not have the motor vehicle.

    A   B   C

4. Gas and air expansion in the combustion chamber occurs when air and fossil fuel are heated.

    A   B   C

5. Internal combustion engines did not replace the steam engine in the 20th century.

    A   B   C

11. Read the following text before answering the questions as either TRUE, FALSE or CANNOT SAY from the information given.

HOW A FRIDGE WORKS

Refrigerators are widely popular everywhere in the world and they are a vital part of any kitchen. If you want to be able to keep food fresh and chilled to the correct temperature, you will need one of these appliances. Not only are they useful, there are also attractive and innovative models that add to the aesthetic appeal of your kitchen. You probably see your fridge multiple times per day but are unaware how it works.

Parts of a Fridge
To understand how a fridge works, first you have to know what parts are inside of it. Every refrigerator has five main components that help it to keep your food and drinks cold. These parts are:

• Exterior heat-exchanging pipes (pipes that are coiled and are outside of the appliance).

• Interior heat-exchanging pipes (pipes that are coiled and are inside of the appliance).

• Compressor.

• Expansion valve.

• Refrigerant (this is a liquid that will evaporate when it is inside the heat-exchanging pipes in the refrigerator, which creates frosty temperatures).

The Cooling Process
When you turn on your fridge, it does not automatically become cold. There are intricate processes at work inside of the appliance. The first thing that happens when your fridge is turned on is that the refrigerant liquid, which is contained within the coils, is compressed into a gas by the compressor. The gas will heat up as it becomes pressurised. The exterior heat-exchange pipes that reside on the rear panel of the unit then lose heat as the hot refrigerant gas dissipates it. The gas will then condense into liquid when it is under this high pressure. This pressurised refrigerant liquid will flow through the expansion valve, which is essentially a very tiny hole. One side of the hole will have the high-pressure liquid, while the other side will have the low-pressure gas that the compressor is pulling from.

Once the liquid flows through the expansion valve, which is essential to the running of the fridge, it will start to boil and turn into a vapour, which drops its temperature. This will cool down the refrigerator. The cold refrigerant gas will then go back through the compressor and the entire process will be repeated.

A – TRUE	B – FALSE	C – CANNOT SAY
Circle A if the question is TRUE from the information provided.	Circle B if the question is FALSE from the information provided.	Circle C if CANNOT SAY from the information provided.

1. Exterior heat-exchanging pipes are located externally on the rear panel.

A   B   C

2. Fridges are commonly known as 'white goods'.

A   B   C

3. In total there are five components to the fridge.

A   B   C

4. Without the expansion valve the fridge will not operate correctly.

A   B   C

5. The refrigerant liquid becomes a gas.

A   B   C

12. Read the following text before answering the questions as either TRUE, FALSE or CANNOT SAY from the information given.

HOW AN AEROPLANES FLIES

There are three principles that you have to understand in order to fully grasp how an aeroplane is able to fly and how it does this effectively. Getting to know The Bernouilli Effect, The Coanda Effect and Newton's Third Law will help you to understand how an aeroplane flies.

The Bernouilli Effect

The Bernouilli Effect explains how the wings enable the aeroplane to fly. The wings are curved into a specific shape to make what is called an air-foil. On the majority of aircrafts, the bottom of the wing (or airfoil) is flat, while the top is a more curved surface. Air will flow very fast over the top because of the shape, which thins this air considerably. This thinner air at the top of the airfoil creates a strong vacuum, which pulls up on the wing. This is how the lifting action is generated and this keeps the aeroplane in the sky.

The Coanda Effect

The Coanda Effect is another force that helps to keep the plane in the air. This is a principle of physics that says that a jet of fluid will most often tend to follow along a curved surface. This is another important factor in keeping the curved wings and body of the plane in the air.

Newton's Third Law

Newton's Third Law explains another reason why an aeroplane will fly. The trailing edge of the wing curves in a downward fashion, so that when air flows over this, it will angle in a downward motion off the wing and shoot out fast behind it. Newton's Third Law of thermodynamics is a principle in physics. It explains that for any action that occurs, there is an opposite and equal reaction to it. As the wing pushes downward and forces are behind it, the air will push the wing upwards. This principle, along with The Bernouilli Effect, explains how an aeroplane will stay in the air. Essentially, it is because of the advanced design of the wings and the body of the plane.

A – TRUE	B – FALSE	C – CANNOT SAY
Circle A if the question is TRUE from the information provided.	Circle B if the question is FALSE from the information provided.	Circle C if CANNOT SAY from the information provided.

1. Millions of people fly on aeroplanes each year.

A   B   C

2. Newton's Third Law is named so because it is the third law in the process of flight.

A   B   C

3. The air flow over the top of a wing is faster than the air flow underneath the wing.

A   B   C

4. The wings on an aeroplane are curved so that the air can flow faster over them.

A   B   C

5. The body of a plane has nothing to do with the aeroplane staying in the air.

A   B   C

Great work! You have now completed the mock exam. Let's now see how well you have done by checking your answers.

ANSWERS AND EXPLANATIONS TO FINAL MOCK EXAM

1. Read the following text before answering the questions as either TRUE, FALSE or CANNOT SAY from the information given.

FACTS ABOUT ANTARCTICA

Very few people ever travel to Antarctica, which is one of the seven continents on the Earth. The reason is because Antarctica is so cold and icy that it is a very inhospitable place for human life. It is a very fascinating place, with lots of amazing wildlife in the surrounding waters.

Some of the many interesting facts about Antarctica include:

- **5: Antarctica, along with the Arctic, is one of the two coldest places on Earth.** It is located very close to the South Pole, while the Arctic is to the north.

- One third of all the fresh water on the entire planet is located on Antarctica.

- There are absolutely no trees on this icy continent.

- **2: The temperature rarely gets above freezing,** so that the entire area is covered in ice and snow. In fact, the ice and snow is one mile deep in most spots and in some areas it is up to three miles deep.

- Very few creatures live on the actual land; in fact the largest creature that resides directly on Antarctica is the midge. Midges are only half an inch long. There are many living creatures in the water surrounding the land, however.

- The lowest temperature ever recorded on Antarctica was in 1983. It was -129 degrees Fahrenheit.

- Codfish in the waters surrounding Antarctica actually have antifreeze flowing through their blood because the water is so cold.

- **1: No single country has claimed ownership over Antarctica.** In fact, all of the countries have agreed to joint ownership and everyone is able to send scientific research missions to the area. **3: No native people reside on the land, as it would be near impossible for humans to live there for an extended period of time.**

> - Many people think of Antarctica as a place where it snows continuously, when it fact it rarely snows each year. Instead, the appearance of snowstorms is caused by existing snow that blows off of the ground by hard winds.
>
> - For a large part of the history of the Earth, Antarctica was a warm continent.
>
> While people do not reside on this ice cold land, some people do go there for research projects and other exploratory missions. **4: It is a vast and beautiful land and much of its beauty is because it is untouched by industrialisation and the damage that humans can inflict.**

A – TRUE	B – FALSE	C – CANNOT SAY
Circle A if the question is TRUE from the information provided.	Circle B if the question is FALSE from the information provided.	Circle C if CANNOT SAY from the information provided.

1. Antarctica is owned by a single country.

A C

The passage states that no single country has claimed ownership of Antarctica; therefore, this statement is **false**.

2. The temperature on Antarctica sometimes rises above freezing.

 B C

The passage informs us that "The temperature **rarely** gets above freezing...". Because of this fact we can accurately state that the temperature does, at some point, rise above freezing. Therefore, the statement is **true**.

3. It is impossible for humans to live on Antarctica for long periods of time.

A  C

The passage states it would be *"**near** impossible for humans to live there for an extended period of time"*. If something is near to being impossible, it cannot be impossible. The statement is **false** based on the information provided in the passage.

4. Antarctica is yet to be affected by industrialisation.

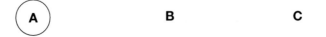

The passage clearly states that Antarctica is "untouched by industrialisation". The statement is **true.**

5. The Arctic is one of the coldest places on Earth.

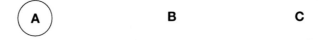

The passage states that "Antarctica, along with the Arctic, is one of the two coldest places on Earth". Therefore, the statement is **true.**

2. Read the following text before answering the questions as either TRUE, FALSE or CANNOT SAY from the information given.

THE QUALITIES OF A GOOD TEACHER

There is no question that teaching is one of the most important careers in the UK. Our teachers are helping to shape the future of our population, as they are training our children to enter the workforce and become the leaders of tomorrow. Without teachers there would be no formal education for our youth in the UK. **3: Many people want to be a teacher, but a large number find that it is just not for them.** Not just anyone can be a good teacher, because it takes certain qualities and personality traits to teach children of all ages.

Those who are the best teachers often have certain aspects to their personalities that enable them to command the attention and respect of their students. **1: Some of the qualities that make up a good teacher include:**

- Patience - **2: Patience is by far the most vital aspect of a teacher's personality.** In order to keep calm and cool when children are misbehaving, a teacher must have extreme patience. **5: This is especially important when handling younger children, as they can often be difficult to control.**

- Intelligence - Of course, in order for a teacher to properly instruct their students, they must be well-versed in the subject that they are teaching. They must be able to give their students the right information and to be prepared to answer any questions that their pupils may come up with.

- Creativity - In order to make lessons more interesting and to engage the students, a teacher must use creativity. Good teachers are able to think of clever ways to present the materials that need to be learned so that children actually want to learn.

- Organisation - Teachers must be organised, as they have a lot of things that they must juggle. They have to keep track of the lessons that they have taught and what they have coming up, they have to keep a hold on papers that they need to grade and they also must have all of the necessary hand-outs for each of their classes.

> • Leadership – Teachers are required to lead their pupils. They must be able to stand in front of the classroom with confidence, so that the children trust and respect them and are willing to be led.
>
> Being a teacher is one of the hardest careers in the world and being good at it is even more challenging. A good teacher will be able to demonstrate all of the above qualities on a daily basis.

A – TRUE	**B – FALSE**	**C – CANNOT SAY**
Circle A if the question is TRUE from the information provided.	Circle B if the question is FALSE from the information provided.	Circle C if CANNOT SAY from the information provided.

1. In total there are five different qualities that make up a good teacher.

A   B   C

The passage states that *"Some of the qualities that make up a good teacher include..."*. Because the sentence in the passage states *'some of the qualities'* we cannot determine exactly how many there are in total. The answer is, therefore, **cannot say**.

2. Patience is not the most important attribute of a teacher's personality.

A   B C

The passage confirms that patience *is* the most vital aspect of a teacher's personality. The statement is **false**.

3. Most people find that teaching is not for them.

A   B   C

The passage states that *"Many people want to be a teacher, but a large number find that it is just not for them"*. The statement makes reference to most people. The passage just states that a **large number** find it is not for them. We cannot decide from the information in the passage whether **a large number** is **'most'** people, therefore, the correct answer is **cannot say.**

4. Teaching is not a particularly well paid job.

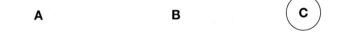

The passage does not make any reference to this claim. The correct answer is **cannot say** based on the information in the passage.

5. Younger children are often the easiest to control.

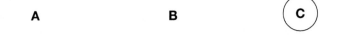

The passage states that younger children can often be difficult to control. You could, therefore, be forgiven for selecting false as the correct answer. In fact, if the question stated – *"Younger children are often **easier** to control"*. The answer would be false.

However, the statement asks us to consider whether or not **"Younger children are often the *easiest* to control"**. There is no information contained in the passage that will help us to confirm that younger children are the **easiest** to control; therefore, the correct answer must be **cannot say**. There is a difference between **easiest** and **easier**.

3. Read the following text before answering the questions as either TRUE, FALSE or CANNOT SAY from the information given.

THE EVOLUTION OF MAN

Evolution is a widely studied science that many scientific leaders have researched and pondered over for many years. **3: For the most part, these scientists believe that human beings evolved from Order Primates. This group includes chimpanzees, monkeys, gorillas and lemurs. They have gathered their information by studying fossils that have been unearthed from all over the world, with the oldest dating back more than 5 million years ago.** Humans evolved because of diet and environmental factors, among other things. Many stages of man have been identified and here we will explain each of them.

The earliest stage of man included such species as Australopithecus anamensis, Australopithecus robustus, Australopithecus africanus and Australopithecus boisei. Australopithecus anamensis is identified as a species that walked on two feet. Australopithecus africanus had a larger brain than other species at the time and seemed to have developed molars and canine teeth, as did the Australopithecus robustus, indicating that both ate things that required more chewing and grinding than before.

Then came along Homo habilis. This species had a much larger brain size than the Australopithecus, which enabled the species to invent tools that they could use for making things and killing prey. Homo habilis may have been able to speak and was about 5 feet tall and weighed around 100 lbs.

1: The next species to come along was Homo erectus, who had an even larger brain size than Hobo habilis. **5: Erectus was also taller (about 5 feet 5 inches) and this is attributed to the fact that he was smarter and able to hunt for meat. The meat made Erectus grow larger and stronger.**

Homo sapiens (Archaic) were next in the evolution of man. Fossils have been found all over the world and scientists can determine from these that he had an even larger brain, which enabled him to reason, speak, make plans and control how he moved his body. He is believed to have been a socialised being that used various weapons and tools.

Homo sapiens neanderthalensis were the next evolution of man, leading to our species today. This species appeared at the very end of the ice age and they were able to survive in very cold weather, because of their body size, which retained more body heat. They had even more social skills than the species before them, as well as a very strong and muscular build. The evolution of man was a long process, over approximately 5 million years, which resulted in the humans that reside on Earth today.

A – TRUE	**B – FALSE**	**C – CANNOT SAY**
Circle A if the question is TRUE from the information provided.	Circle B if the question is FALSE from the information provided.	Circle C if CANNOT SAY from the information provided.

1. Homo erectus evolved prior to Homo habilis.

A B C

The passage confirms that Homo erectus came after Homo habilis. The statement is **false**.

2. Homo sapiens were capable of controlling their own body movement.

A B C

The information in the passage confirms that Homo sapiens were capable of controlling how the body moved. The statement is **true.**

3. The human race is more than 5 million years old.

A B C

The passage states that scientists **believe** that human beings evolved from Order Primates. It goes on to state that Order Primates include chimpanzees, monkeys, gorillas and lemurs. It then moves on to disclose that scientists have gathered their information by studying fossils with the oldest dating back to more than 5 million years old.

Because the passage states that scientists **believe** the human race evolved from Order Primates, there is nothing to confirm in the passage that their **belief** is fact. Therefore, we **cannot say** if the statement is true or false based on the information provided.

4. Homo habilis was able to speak.

A   B   C

The passage states that Homo habilis **may** have been able to speak. We **cannot say** whether this claim is true or false based on the information in the passage.

5. Homo erectus was capable of eating meat.

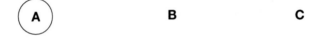

A   B   C

The passage states that Homo erectus grew stronger and taller because of meat. The statement is **true.**

4. Read the following text before answering the questions as either TRUE, FALSE or CANNOT SAY from the information given.

THE DIFFERENCE BETWEEN AFFECT AND EFFECT

Not everyone is skilled with grammar and even those who are struggle with some of the most commonly mistaken words in the English language. Two words that cause a lot of confusion for people are affect and effect. Many people have a lot of trouble with the usage and the meanings of these words, as they are very easy to mix up. The majority of people aren't really sure of when to use one or the other, which is why they simply end up guessing.

The reason why these two words are so confusing is that while each is a different part of speech, they sometimes function as other parts of speech. **1: In most cases, affect is a verb and effect is a noun. 2: You can affect something, which will produce an effect on that thing.** Things are always affected, never effected. This is the general rule that you should always remember. Only in rare cases will affect or effect serve as different parts of speech. **4: Remember that an effect is always something that is produced and an affect is what you do to something.**

Just to be thoroughly confusing, there are very rare situations when effect will be used as a verb and affect will be used as a noun. For the most part, you will never have to use them in these cases. Use the general rule from above (affect is a verb and effect is a noun), but try to remember the following odd instances. As a verb, effect means to accomplish, produce or execute something. As a noun, affect is used by psychologists to refer to desires and emotions as factors in how someone acts or thinks. Obviously, both of these instances do not occur often, but you will see them sometimes in things you may be reading, such as an academic journal. Always keep in your mind that under most circumstances, use affect as a verb and effect as a noun.

A – TRUE	B – FALSE	C – CANNOT SAY
Circle A if the question is TRUE from the information provided.	Circle B if the question is FALSE from the information provided.	Circle C if CANNOT SAY from the information provided.

1. In most cases, effect is a verb and affect is a noun.

A   

The passage states *"In most cases, **affect** is a verb and **effect** is a noun"*. Did you notice that affect and effect had been swapped around in the statement? Therefore, the statement is **false.**

2. If something is affected there will be a resultant effect on it.

      B   C

The passage states that *"You can affect something, which will produce an effect on that thing"*. The statement is **true.**

3. There are occasions when effect will be used as a verb and affect will be used as a noun.

   B   C

"Just to be thoroughly confusing, there are very rare situations when effect will be used as a verb and affect will be used as a noun." The statement is **true.**

4. Affect can be described as what you do to something.

   B   C

The passage confirms that affect is what you do to something. The statement is **true.**

5. Affect is always something that is produced and an effect is what you do to something.

A   **B** **C**

Unless you read the passage carefully you could quite easily select true as your answer. The passage states that *"effect is always something that is produced and an affect is what you do to something"*. The statement is **false.**

5. Read the following text before answering the questions as either TRUE, FALSE or CANNOT SAY from the information given.

MOUNT EVEREST

1: Mount Everest is one of the most famous natural landmarks in the world; it is the highest point above sea level on Earth. Many mountain climbers seek to climb Mount Everest as their ultimate goal and people visit in droves every single year to test their climbing skills on this peak. Here are some facts about Mount Everest to help you understand more about the mountain and its history.

- Everest is about 29,000 feet above sea level.

- The mountain was actually named by British surveyors for George Everest. **5: He was a famous Surveyor General of India throughout the mid-nineteenth century.**

- Everest has been altered considerably by five major glaciers, which still continue to change how the mountain looks. Glaciers have been credited with turning the mountain into a massive pyramid with three large ridges and three faces. **1: The best time to climb Everest is at the beginning of May. This will ensure that the monsoon season is avoided.**

- In 1975, the largest expedition to climb Everest was completed. A group of 410 people from China scaled the mountain together.

- One of the biggest problems that people face when climbing Everest is the extreme climate. The temperatures on the mountain never get above freezing and in the dead of winter they are well within negative temperatures. Climbers have to prepare not only for the lack of oxygen at altitude, but also for the incredibly cold temperatures.

- **2: Everest is rising 1/3 of an inch every single year.** It is also very slowly moving northeastward, at about 3 inches per year.

- Climbers Peter Habeler and Reinhold Messner have the distinction of being the first people to climb the mountain without supplemental oxygen. They did this in 1978.

- The safest year for climbers on Mount Everest was 1993. This is because 129 climbers made it all the way to the summit, with 8 deaths.

- 1996 is considered the least safe year on the mountain. 98 climbers made it to the summit, yet 15 died.

- The mountain is considered very sacred by those in Tibet and Nepal. **3: In Tibet, Mount Everest is called Chomolangma, which means 'Goddess Mother of Snows', in the Tibetan language.** Those in Nepal refer to the mountain as Sagarmatha, which means *'Mother of the Universe'*.

A – TRUE	**B – FALSE**	**C – CANNOT SAY**
Circle A if the question is TRUE from the information provided.	Circle B if the question is FALSE from the information provided.	Circle C if CANNOT SAY from the information provided.

1. The monsoon season starts after the month of May.

A   B   **C**

The passage states that by climbing Everest at the beginning of May you will avoid the monsoon season. We cannot tell from this information if the monsoon season is before the month of May or after it. Therefore, the correct answer is **cannot say**.

2. Everest is increasing in height each year.

A   B   C

From the information provided in the passage this statement is **true**.

3. To some people in Nepal, Mount Everest is also called Chomolangma, which means 'Goddess Mother of Snows'.

A   **B** C

The passage states *"In Tibet, Mount Everest is called Chomolangma, which means 'Goddess Mother of Snows',* in the Tibetan language. The statement is **false** as it mentions people in Nepal, as opposed to Tibet.

4. Everest is the tallest mountain in the world.

The passage states that Mount Everest is the highest point above sea level on Earth; therefore, it would be prudent to assume that it is the tallest mountain in the world. However, our task is not to assume and the correct answer is **cannot say** from the information provided.

5. George Everest worked in India during the mid-nineteenth century.

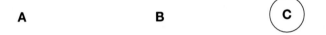

Although the passage states that George Everest was a famous Surveyor General of India throughout the mid-nineteenth century, it does not confirm whether or not he actually lived there. There, the answer is **cannot say.**

6. Read the following text before answering the questions as either TRUE, FALSE or CANNOT SAY from the information given.

THE CAMINO DE SANTIAGO

The Camino de Santiago was a major Christian pilgrimage route to the Cathedral of Santiago de Compostela in northwestern Spain. It dates back to medieval times and is still in existence today. This historic pilgrimage route has many interesting and unique things about it. Here are some facts and figures related to the Camino de Santiago:

- In English, The Camino de Santiago means The Way of Saint James, which is how many in the English-speaking world refer to this historic route.

- The Camino has been a Christian route for more than 1,000 years and many believe that it was used for other purposes long before that.

- The Camino was named as the very first European Cultural Route in 1987 by the Council of Europe. It is also one of UNESCO's World Heritage Sites.

- The symbol of the Camino de Santiago is the scallop shell. There are differing stories as to why, but many believe it is because the shell has multiple grooves that come together at a single point. This is a metaphor for how people came down many paths to end up at the Camino de Santiago.

- **5: The earliest records of visitors to the Cathedral date back all the way to the 8th century.**

- 4: Pilgrims who travelled the route purchased a "credencial", or pilgrim's passport, from the Spanish government so that they could safely travel the route. They could show their passport at various pilgrim's hostels along the way in Spain and France, where they could stay overnight.

- **1: Pilgrims who completed the walk along the Camino de Santiago were given a certificate of accomplishment called the Compostela. 3: They had to walk at least 100 km in order to achieve this, but it was a very big honour for the devout people that had travelled to the Cathedral.**

- Every day at noon, a pilgrim's mass is held at the Cathedral of Santiago de Compostela in honour of the pilgrims.

- On special Holy Years, more pilgrims than ever take the route. The last Holy Year was 2010, when more than 272,000 pilgrims walked the route to the Cathedral. **2: The next Holy Year is in 2021.** Holy Years are when the sacred holiday of Saint James's Day (July 25), falls on a Sunday.

The Camino de Santiago is a very famous and historical route that people today still travel to get to the Cathedral of Santiago de Compostela.

A – TRUE	**B – FALSE**	**C – CANNOT SAY**
Circle A if the question is TRUE from the information provided.	Circle B if the question is FALSE from the information provided.	Circle C if CANNOT SAY from the information provided.

1. Pilgrims are the people who walk the Camino de Santiago.

A   B   C

The passage confirms that *"Pilgrims who completed the walk along the Camino de Santiago were given a certificate of accomplishment called the Compostela"*. The answer is **true.**

2. The next Holy Year will be 2012.

A    B C

The passage states the next Holy Year will be 2021. The statement is **false.**

3. The Camino de Santiago is 100 km long.

A   B   C

The passage only makes reference to the fact that pilgrims had to walk at least 100km of the Camino de Santiago in order to receive their certificate of accomplishment. It makes no reference to how long the route is; therefore, the correct answer is **cannot say** based on the information provided.

4. A credencial is a pilgrim's passport that enables them to travel safely.

According to the passage this statement is **true.**

5. People have been walking the Camino de Santiago since the 8th century.

The passage states that *"The earliest records of visitors to the Cathedral date back all the way to the 8th century"*. This only confirms that visitors to the Cathedral date back to the 8th century and not actual walkers of the route. Therefore, we **cannot say** based on the information provided.

7. Read the following text before answering the questions as either TRUE, FALSE or CANNOT SAY from the information given.

THE EUROPEAN UNION

The European Union was officially established in 1993 under its current name. The history of the EU and its current actions are something that many people are not fully aware of. Here are some interesting facts and figures about the European Union.

- The Maastricht Treaty of 1993 formally named the European Union.

- The EU traces its roots all the way back to European Coal and Steel Community and the European Economic Community, formed together by six member countries in 1958.

- **3: The EU has a combined population of 500 million inhabitants in 27 member states. This is 7.3% of the world's population.**

- The eurozone, which is a monetary union within the European Union, was established in 1999. **5: There are 17 member states in the eurozone, all of which utilise the euro as their form of currency. This enables free spending in all of the eurozone countries without having to exchange currencies, making movement from country to country much easier.**

- There are many important institutions of the EU, such as the European Commission, Council of the European Union, the European Council, the European Central Bank, and the Court Justice of the European Union.

- European Parliament is part of the legislative function of the EU and members are directly elected from each member country every 5 years.

- The anthem of the European Union is "Ode to Joy".

- In the entire organisation there are 23 different languages spoken.

- **1: The euro currency was introduced on January 1, 2002, where it was printed and distributed throughout 12 member countries. This was a huge logistical operation, with nearly 80 billion coins involved.**

- 38,000 people are employed by the European Commission.

- 1% of the annual budget of the EU is spent on staff and administration, as well as continued maintenance on buildings.

- The European Commission is hailed as having one of the largest translation centres in the world, with 1,750 linguists. There are also 600 support staff members for the linguists.

- European Parliament holds its regular committee meetings in Brussels.

- **2: The EU has the world's third largest population, after China and India.**

- The EU's GDP is now bigger than that of the US.

The European Union has certainly grown immensely since it was officially named in 1993. 12 member states were added since 2004 and the population and economic impact continues to grow.

A – TRUE	B – FALSE	C – CANNOT SAY
Circle A if the question is TRUE from the information provided.	Circle B if the question is FALSE from the information provided.	Circle C if CANNOT SAY from the information provided.

1. There are currently 12 countries using the euro currency.

A B **C**

The passage only confirms that the currency was distributed amongst 12 member states countries in 2002. It does not confirm how many countries are using the currency currently. Therefore, we **cannot say** based on the information provided.

2. There are more people living in the European Union than China.

A B C

The passage confirms that *"The EU has the world's third largest population, after China and India"*. The answer is **false** as there are more people living in China than the European Union.

3. 7.3% of the world's population live in the European Union.

                    B   **C**

According to the passage, this statement is **true.**

4. Greece is in the European Union.

    A   **B**   **C**

The passage makes no mention of Greece being in the European Union. Therefore, we **cannot say** based on the information provided.

5. One of the benefits of the eurozone is that it negates the need to change currency between the different countries that form part of it.

    A   **B**   **C**

The passage states *"There are 17 member states in the eurozone, all of which utilise the euro as their form of currency. This enables free spending in all of the eurozone countries without having to exchange currencies, making movement from country to country much easier".* The passage confirms that the statement is **true**.

8. Read the following text before answering the questions as either TRUE, FALSE or CANNOT SAY from the information given.

RULES OF AMERICAN FOOTBALL

American football is an incredibly popular sport all over the United States, but it is less popular throughout other countries. An increasing number of people in the UK are starting to play and watch this classic American sport. If you want to be able to play, or understand the sport while watching it on television, you need to know the rules. Here is an overview of the basic rules of American football.

Offense and Defense
Each team has 11 players on the field at one time. The team that has possession of the football is the offense, and their objective is to advance the ball down the field. They do this by running with the ball, or passing it to another team-mate. They score points when they get to the very end of the field, crossing the goal line into the end zone. The team that does not have the ball is the defense. Their objective is to prevent the other team from getting into the end zone and scoring a touchdown. They do this by attempting to block players from catching passes, tackling players who are running with the ball, and/or trying to catch passes that are intended for the offensive team (catching such a pass is called an interception).

2: If the offensive team scores, or if they lose possession of the ball to the defense, then the two teams switch roles. This continues on until the four timed quarters of the game have been completed. **The game is divided into four 15-minute quarters, along with a half-time break of 12 minutes. The teams change ends of the field after each quarter.**

The Field
5: A football field measures 100 yards long and is 53 yard wide. There are markers on the field to tell the players, coaches and officials which yard line they are on. Every 10 yards is marked by a line. The end zone is also marked and is at the 0-yard line on the field. This zone is 10 yards long, but does not count towards the 100 yards of the field.

Moving the Ball Down the Field
The offensive team must do their best to gain as much 'yardage' before they are stopped by a tackle or an out of bounds movement. With each ten yards the offense progresses, they get what is called a first down.

If they pass the ball and it is incomplete or someone fumbles and they do not gain any yards, this is a second down. The team has four tries (or downs) to get the ball down the field before they must give up possession. If they are on their second, third or fourth down and make it 10 yards, they start over at a first down.

Scoring
1 & 5: If the offense makes it to the end zone, they score a touch-down, which is six points. They can then either kick a field goal for an extra point, or they can do a small play in the last 10 yards of the field which is called a two-point conversion and is worth two points. If they do not score a touchdown and decide to try for a field goal, they can score three points. There are many other intricate rules of American football, but the above are all of the most important aspects.

A – TRUE	**B – FALSE**	**C – CANNOT SAY**
Circle A if the question is TRUE from the information provided.	Circle B if the question is FALSE from the information provided.	Circle C if CANNOT SAY from the information provided.

1. In American Football you can only score points via a touchdown when the ball crosses the goal line into the end zone.

                    B   C

The statement is **false** as there are alternative ways to score points other than a touchdown in the end zone.

2. When a team does not have the ball they are the defense.

       A   B   C

The passage states that *"If the offensive team scores, or if they lose possession of the ball to the defense, then the two teams switch roles."* The statement is **true**.

3. The game of American Football, excluding breaks, is 60 minutes in duration.

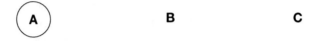

A   B   C

The passage states *"The game is divided into four 15-minute quarters, along with a half-time break of 12 minutes. The teams change ends of the field after each quarter."* Therefore, the total duration of the game, excluding breaks, is 60 minutes. The statement is **true.**

4. The protective helmets worn by American Footballers are designed to protect the head from injury.

A   B   C

The passage makes no reference to the helmets that are worn by the players, or their intended purpose. The correct answer is **cannot say** based on the information provided.

5. A football field measures 100 yards wide and 53 yards long.

A   C

The passage states that the length is 100 yards and the width is 53 yards. The answer is **false.**

9. Read the following text before answering the questions as either TRUE, FALSE or CANNOT SAY from the information given.

FACTS ABOUT THE NATIONAL GEOGRAPHIC

2: The National Geographic Society (NGS) is a group that is head-quartered in Washington, DC in the United States, which publishes a magazine titled National Geographic. The group and the fascinating magazine it releases are very interesting to many people all over the world, as they have made huge strides in environmental and historical preservation, among other things.

- **4: The National Geographic Society was founded on January 27, 1888 by Gardiner Greene Hubbard.**

- **3: Worldwide membership of the society is currently at about 8.5 million people.**

- The current president since 1998 is John M. Fahey, Jr.

- The logo for the NGS is a rectangular yellow portrait frame, which can be found as its television logo and on the margins surrounding the front cover of their magazine.

- **5: The organisation is designed to fund research and preservation of historical, archaeological, and natural science areas throughout the entire world. It is a non-profit organisation.**

- The Society has given grants for scientific research since it began, and recently gave out its 10,000th grant.

- The NGS began as a group for elite world travellers and academics that were wealthy and interested in advancing tourism and interest in history, science and culture.

- In 2004, the NGS headquarters in Washington, DC was one of the first buildings ever to receive a Green Certification from Global Green USA.

- The magazine started nine months after the society was founded in October 1888. It is published 12 times per year, along with at least four supplements.

- **1: More than 50 million readers all over the world read National Geographic every month, in 32 different languages.**

- NGS has funded more than 9,600 conservation, research and exploration projects throughout the entire Earth.

- In addition to the magazine, NGS reaches more than 400 million people per month through videos, their television channel, books, radio, music, films, interactive media and more.

- National Geographic won the 'Magazine of the Year' award from the American Society of Magazine Editors in 2011, the top award any magazine can receive.

- The magazine has tackled such issues as environmentalism, endangered species, global warming, chemical pollution, deforestation and so much more.

- National Geographic has held an annual photography competition since 2006, with people competing in 18 different countries.

A – TRUE	B – FALSE	C – CANNOT SAY
Circle A if the question is TRUE from the information provided.	Circle B if the question is FALSE from the information provided.	Circle C if CANNOT SAY from the information provided.

1. More than 50 million readers all over the world read National Geographic every year, in 32 different languages.

  A **B** **C**

The passage states that *"More than 50 million readers all over the world read National Geographic every **month**, in 32 different languages"*. The statement, however, is slightly different as it states every **year**. If there are more than 50 million readers every month then there are more than 50 million readers every year. The statement is **true**.

2. The National Geographic Society's magazine is not titled National Geographic.

A  **B** **C**

According to the passage this statement is **false**. The magazine is titled National Geographic.

3. The National Geographic Society has 50 million members all over the world in 32 different languages.

A   B) C

The statement is **false**. The passage confirms that the "Worldwide membership of the society is currently at about 8.5 million people."

4. The National Geographic Society was founded over 100 years ago.

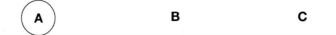

A   B   C

The passage states *"The National Geographic Society was founded on January 27, 1888 by Gardiner Greene Hubbard"*. Therefore, the statement is **true** as the society was founded over 100 years ago.

5. The National Geographic Society is a profitable business.

A   B) C

The passage states that the National Geographic is a non-profit organisation. The statement is **false.**

10. Read the following text before answering the questions as either TRUE, FALSE or CANNOT SAY from the information given.

INTERNAL COMBUSTION ENGINE THEORY

Internal combustion engines are the most commonly used engines in the entire world. They are used in a wide range of vehicles and chances are if you drive a car, yours uses this type of engine. **5: They are also used in industrial applications and largely replaced the steam engine throughout the 20th century.**

What is the theory?
The main principle behind any type of internal combustion engine is if you put a small amount of a type of high-energy fuel, such as gasoline, into a very small space and ignite it, a large amount of energy will be released in the form of gas that expands. This energy can then be used to propel almost anything and it is very effective. **1: This is why the majority of common vehicle engines are built based upon this theory.** This principle is the core that most car engines today are built on.

How it works
The engine utilises a fossil fuel inside of a combustion chamber and combines this with an oxidiser, which is usually air. **4: When the air and the fossil fuel are heated in the combustion chamber, the gas and the air will expand.** The expansion of the gas and the air when combustion is applied causes a force to the pistons, turbine blades, or nozzle inside of the engine. This then transforms the chemical energy of the internal combustion energy into mechanical energy that powers the vehicle or industrial application.

Most cars on the roads right now use a four-stroke combustion cycle. This converts gasoline so that it can propel the car forward. This is also called the 'Otto Cycle', as it is named after the inventor, Nikolaus Otto, who invented it in 1867. These four strokes are called the intake stroke, compression stroke, combustion stroke, and the exhaust stroke.

2: The first internal combustion engine was created by Jean Joseph Étienne Lenoir, a Belgian engineer, in 1859. 3: Without his application of the theory, we might not have the advanced vehicle engines we have today.

A – TRUE	**B – FALSE**	**C – CANNOT SAY**
Circle A if the question is TRUE from the information provided.	Circle B if the question is FALSE from the information provided.	Circle C if CANNOT SAY from the information provided.

1. The majority of vehicle engines are built based upon the internal combustion engine theory.

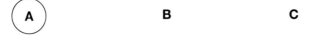

The passage confirms this statement to be **true.**

2. The first internal combustion engine was built in Belgium.

The passage states *"The first internal combustion engine was created by Jean Joseph Étienne Lenoir, a Belgian engineer, in 1859".* Although the passage indicates that the creator of the first internal combustion engine was a Belgian engineer, this does not confirm that the first engine was actually **built** in Belgium. Therefore, we **cannot say** without further information whether the statement is true or false.

3. Without the internal combustion engine we would not have the motor vehicle.

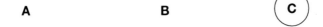

The passage states *"Without his application of the theory, we might not have the advanced vehicle engines we have today".* There is a difference between 'might not have' and 'would not have'. The correct answer is **cannot say** without further information.

4. Gas and air expansion in the combustion chamber occurs when air and fossil fuel are heated.

The statement is **true** because the passage states *"When the air and the fossil fuel are heated in the combustion chamber, the gas and the air will expand"*.

5. Internal combustion engines did not replace the steam engine in the 20th century.

The passage states *"They are also used in industrial applications and largely replaced the steam engine throughout the 20th century"*. Whilst they largely replaced steam engines the passage does not say they replaced them entirely. The statement is **false.**

11. Read the following text before answering the questions as either TRUE, FALSE or CANNOT SAY from the information given.

HOW A FRIDGE WORKS

Refrigerators are widely popular everywhere in the world and they are a vital part of any kitchen. If you want to be able to keep food fresh and chilled to the correct temperature, you will need one of these appliances. Not only are they useful, there are also attractive and innovative models that add to the aesthetic appeal of your kitchen. You probably see your fridge multiple times per day but are unaware how it works.

Parts of a Fridge
To understand how a fridge works, first you have to know what parts are inside of it. **3: Every refrigerator has five main components that help it to keep your food and drinks cold.** These parts are:

- Exterior heat-exchanging pipes (pipes that are coiled and are outside of the appliance).

- Interior heat-exchanging pipes (pipes that are coiled and are inside of the appliance).

- Compressor.

- Expansion valve.

- Refrigerant (this is a liquid that will evaporate when it is inside the heat-exchanging pipes in the refrigerator, which creates frosty temperatures).

The Cooling Process
When you turn on your fridge, it does not automatically become cold. There are intricate processes at work inside of the appliance. **5: The first thing that happens when your fridge is turned on is that the refrigerant liquid, which is contained within the coils, is compressed into a gas by the compressor.** The gas will heat up as it becomes pressurised. **1: The exterior heat-exchange pipes that reside on the rear panel of the unit then lose heat as the hot refrigerant gas dissipates it.** The gas will then condense into liquid when it is under this high pressure. This pressurised refrigerant liquid will flow through the expansion valve, which is essentially a very tiny hole. One side of the hole will have the high-pressure liquid, while the other side will have the low-pressure gas that the compressor is pulling from.

> **4: Once the liquid flows through the expansion valve, which is essential to the running of the fridge, it will start to boil and turn into a vapour, which drops its temperature.** This will cool down the refrigerator. The cold refrigerant gas will then go back through the compressor and the entire process will be repeated.

A – TRUE	B – FALSE	C – CANNOT SAY
Circle A if the question is TRUE from the information provided.	Circle B if the question is FALSE from the information provided.	Circle C if CANNOT SAY from the information provided.

1. Exterior heat-exchanging pipes are located externally on the rear panel.

    B   C

The passage states *"The **exterior heat-exchange pipes that reside on the rear panel** of the unit then lose heat as the hot refrigerant gas dissipates it"*. The statement is **true** based on this information.

2. Fridges are commonly known as 'white goods'.

A   B   C

Although this statement is true in everyday life, the passage makes no reference to it. We **cannot say** based on the information provided.

3. In total there are five components to the fridge.

A   B   C

Although the passage states that there are 5 main components, it does not confirm that these are the **total** number of components. The answer is **cannot say** without further information.

4. Without the expansion valve the fridge will not operate correctly.

The passage confirms that the expansion valve is essential to the running of the fridge; therefore, the statement is **true.**

5. The refrigerant liquid becomes a gas.

"The first thing that happens when your fridge is turned on is that the refrigerant liquid, which is contained within the coils, is compressed into a gas by the compressor." The statement is **true** based on the information provided in the passage.

12. Read the following text before answering the questions as either TRUE, FALSE or CANNOT SAY from the information given.

HOW AN AEROPLANES FLIES

There are three principles that you have to understand in order to fully grasp how an aeroplane is able to fly and how it does this effectively. Getting to know The Bernouilli Effect, The Coanda Effect and Newton's Third Law will help you to understand how an aeroplane flies.

The Bernouilli Effect

The Bernouilli Effect explains how the wings enable the aeroplane to fly. **4: The wings are curved into a specific shape to make what is called an airfoil. On the majority of aircrafts, the bottom of the wing (or airfoil) is flat, while the top is a more curved surface. 3: Air will flow very fast over the top because of the shape, which thins this air considerably.** This thinner air at the top of the airfoil creates a strong vacuum, which pulls up on the wing. This is how the lifting action is generated and this keeps the aeroplane in the sky.

The Coanda Effect

The Coanda Effect is another force that helps to keep the plane in the air. This is a principle of physics that says that a jet of fluid will most often tend to follow along a curved surface. This is another important factor in keeping the curved wings and body of the plane in the air.

Newton's Third Law

Newton's Third Law explains another reason why an aeroplane will fly. The trailing edge of the wing curves in a downward fashion, so that when air flows over this, it will angle in a downward motion off the wing and shoot out fast behind it. Newton's Third Law of thermodynamics is a principle in physics. It explains that for any action that occurs, there is an opposite and equal reaction to it. As the wing pushes downward and forces are behind it, the air will push the wing upwards. **5: This principle, along with The Bernouilli Effect, explains how an aeroplane will stay in the air. Essentially, it is because of the advanced design of the wings and the body of the plane.**

A –TRUE	**B – FALSE**	**C – CANNOT SAY**
Circle A if the question is TRUE from the information provided.	Circle B if the question is FALSE from the information provided.	Circle C if CANNOT SAY from the information provided.

1. Millions of people fly on aeroplanes each year.

A   B   C

There is nothing in the passage to confirm this statement. The correct answer is **cannot say** without further information.

2. Newton's Third Law is named so because it is the third law in the process of flight.

A   B   C

Once again, there is nothing in the passage to confirm this statement. Just because the law is listed third in the passage sequence does not mean the law is the third one in the process of flight. The correct answer is **cannot say** without further information.

3. The air flow over the top of a wing is faster than the air flow underneath the wing.

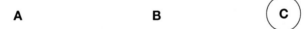

A   B   C

The passage does confirm that air will flow very fast over the top. However, it does not confirm that air flowing over the top of the wing is faster that the flow underneath the wing. The correct answer is **cannot say** based on the information provided.

4. The wings on an aeroplane are curved so that the air can flow faster over them.

A   B   C

The passage states *"The wings are curved into a specific shape to make what is called an airfoil. On the majority of aircrafts, the bottom of the wing (or airfoil) is flat, while the top is a more curved surface"*.

The passage then goes on to state *"Air will flow very fast over the top because of the shape, which thins this air considerably"*.

From the information in the two paragraphs above the statement is **true.**

5. The body of a plane has nothing to do with the aer oplane staying in the air.

The passage states *"This principle, along with The Bernouilli Effect, explains how an aeroplane will stay in the air. Essentially, it is because of the advanced design of the wings **and the body of the plane"**.

The statement is **false** because the body of the plane does have something to do with the aeroplane staying in the air.

HOW DID YOU SCORE?

44 – 50 = Excellent

35 – 43 = Above average

25 – 34 = Average

16 – 24 = Below average

0 – 15 = Well below average

A FEW FINAL WORDS

Congratulations on reaching the end of the workbook. Before I sign off, I want to provide you with some details about what your results mean and how an employer will use them to assess you for the position you are applying for.

WHAT IS A GOOD SCORE?

It is difficult to pinpoint what constitutes a good score. The reason for this is because the majority of employers will use your scores in the verbal reasoning test in **conjunction** with your scores from any other element of assessment/testing you are required to undertake as part of the selection process. In addition to sitting a verbal reasoning test you will most probably be required to sit other testing elements such as a numerical reasoning test, a group exercise and an interview.

The assessor/employer will also compare your test marks against those who have previously sat the test. This is often referred to as a comparison group. It is now more common for an assessor to grade your scores in the test compared to the previous **comparison group**, as opposed to giving you a definitive score. For example, you could be graded as follows:

Your scores are well above average compared to previous test takers in this category.

Your scores are above average compared to previous test takers in this category.

Your scores are in the average range for those who have previously sat this test.

Your scores are below average compared to previous test takers in this category.

If you have performed **above average** scores during the final mock exam you are certainly on the way to gaining a good score in your actual test.

Thank you for choosing How2become as your source of help and preparation for your verbal reasoning tests. Good luck with all your future tests and career moves.

Visit www.how2become.co.uk to find more career testing titles:

- How to pass any career selection process
- Online psychometric testing facilities
- How to pass any job interview
- 1-day intensive training courses

how2become.co.uk

THE **TESTING** SERIES